Parenting
YOUNG CHILDREN

Systematic Training for Effective Parenting (STEP) of Children Under Six

Don Dinkmeyer, Sr.
Gary D. McKay
James S. Dinkmeyer
Don Dinkmeyer, Jr.
Joyce L. McKay

STEP Publishers
STEP into Parenting

www.STEPPublishers.com
800-720-1286

To all the parents and leaders of Early Childhood STEP, and to Rudolf Dreikurs—our teacher, friend, and source of encouragement.

Together, we are meeting our responsibility and challenge: Parent education is the right of every child.

Chapter 1: Some information on temperament is from Stella Chess and Alexander Thomas, *Know Your Child: An Authoritative Guide for Today's Parents* (New York: Basic Books, 1987); on relationships with grandparents is from T. Berry Brazelton, *Touchpoints* (Reading, MA: Addison-Wesley, 1992); on important adults is from Burton White, *The New First Three Years of Life* (New York: Fireside, 1995).

Chapter 2: Tips for avoiding the traps of birth order come from Kathy Walton of the Adlerian Child Care Centers in Columbia, SC; the four goals of misbehavior originated in Rudolf Dreikurs and Vicki Soltz, *Children the Challenge* (New York: Dutton, 1987)

Chapter 3: Some information on the importance of self-esteem is from Dorothy Corkille Briggs, *Your Child's Self-Esteem: The Key to His Life* (New York: Doubleday, Dolphin Books, 1975); on responding with understanding and focusing on strengths and efforts is from Don Dinkmeyer and Lewis L. Losoncy, *The Skills of Encouragement* (Delray Beach, FL: St. Lucie's Press, 1996); on arranging child care is from Helen Neville and Mona Halaby, *No-Fault Parenting* (Tucson, AZ: The Body Press, 1984), and from Sue Bredekamp and Carol Copple, eds., *Developmentally Appropriate Practice in Early Childhood Programs,* rev. ed. (Washington, DC: the National Association for the Education of Young Children, 1997). The concept of the courage to be imperfect comes from Rudolf Dreikurs.

Chapter 4: Information on reflective listening and saying no is from Stanley Greenspan and Nancy Thorndike Greenspan, *First Feelings* (New York: Viking Penguin, 1989); I-messages are from Thomas Gordon, *P.E.T.: Parent Effectiveness Training* (New York: NAL-Dutton, 1975).

Chapter 5: Some information on expecting cooperation is from Don Dinkmeyer and Gary D. Mckay, *Raising a Responsible Child,* rev. ed. (New York: Fireside, 1996) and on negativism in toddlers is from Fitzhugh Dodson, *How to Parent* (New York: New American Library, 1973). Problem ownership is from Thomas Gordon, *P.E.T.: Parent Effectiveness Training* (New York: NAL-Dutton, 1975).

Chapter 6: Some information on childproofing is from Benjamin Spock and Michael B. Rothenberg, *Dr. Spock's Baby and Child Care,* 40th anniversary ed. (New York: NAL-Dutton, 1985); on children's need for control, different rules, and noticing the positive is from Stanley Greenspan and Nancy Thorndike Greenspan, *First Feelings* (New York: Viking Penguin, 1989).

Chapter 7: Some information on sadness, fears, physical symptoms of stress, toilet training, and bedtime is from T. Berry Brazelton, *Touchpoints* (Reading, MA: Addison-Wesley, 1992); on parent fears is from Stanley Greenspan and Nancy Thorndike Greenspan, *First Feelings* (New York: Viking Penguin, 1989); on temper tantrums is from T. Berry Brazelton, *What Every Baby Knows* (New York: Ballantine, 1988); on independence is from T. Berry Brazelton, *Toddlers and Parents,* rev. ed. (New York: Dell, 1989); on depression and empathy is from Daniel Goleman, *Emotional Intelligence* (New York: Bantam Books, 1995); on raising emotionally intelligent children is from John Gottman, *The Heart of Parenting* (Simon and Schuster, 1997).

Photo Credits: Cheryl Walsh Bellville Photography: pp. 74, 114. Myrleen Ferguson Cate, PhotoEdit: p. vi. Elizabeth Crews, The Image Works: pp. 9, 65. Don Dinkmeyer, Jr.: p. 3. Larry Douglas, amwest: p. 107. Thomas Edwards, Third Coast: p. 18. Svat Macha, amwest: p. 23. Julie Nauman: p. 99. Michael Neveux, Westlight: p. 40. Steve Niedorf, Niedorf Photography: pp. 24, 25, 44, 105, 117, 124. Alan Oddie, PhotoEdit: pp. 5, 60. H. Armstrong Roberts, cover; David Shaffer, Shaffer Photography: p. 69. James L. Shaffer, Shaffer Photography: pp. 78, 87, 103. Michael Siluk: p. 51. Charles Thatcher, Tony Stone: p. 92. Topham, The Image Works: p. 46.

Marjorie Lisovskis, Writer/Editor; Evans McCormick, Creative Design/Typesetting; John Bush, cartoons.

www.STEPPublishers.com

Printed in the United States of America

ISBN 978-0-9795542-3-0

A 0 9 8 7 6

Contents

Other Works by the Authors

The Effective Parent (Don Dinkmeyer, Gary D. McKay, Don Dinkmeyer, Jr., James S. Dinkmeyer, and Joyce L. McKay)

The Parent's Handbook (Don Dinkmeyer, Sr., Gary D. McKay, and Don Dinkmeyer, Jr.)

Parenting Teenagers: Systematic Training for Effective Parenting of Teens (Don Dinkmeyer and Gary D. McKay)

Systematic Training for Effective Teaching (STET) (Don Dinkmeyer Sr., Gary D. McKay and Don Dinkmeyer, Jr.)

Preparing Responsible and Effective Parents (PREP) (Don Dinkmeyer, Sr., Gary D. McKay, Don Dinkmeyer, Jr., James S. Dinkmeyer, and Jon Carlson)

Time for a Better Marriage (Don Dinkmeyer and Jon Carlson)

Raising a Responsible Child: How to Prepare Your Child for Today's Complex World (Don Dinkmeyer and Gary D. McKay)

Taking Time for Love: How to Stay Happily Married (Don Dinkmeyer and Jon Carlson)

The Encouragement Book (Don Dinkmeyer and Lewis E. Losoncy)

The Skills of Encouragement (Don Dinkmeyer and Lewis E. Losoncy)

Leadership by Encouragement (Don Dinkmeyer and Daniel Eckstein)

How You Feel Is Up to You: The Power of Emotional Choice (Gary D. McKay and Don Dinkmeyer)

Consultation in the Schools (Don Dinkmeyer, Jr. and Jon Carlson)

Introduction

Being a parent is both a joy and a challenge. No amount of planning or foresight can totally prepare you for the new world that awaits you with your first baby. When that baby arrives, your life is forever changed. You form a major love relationship with an unknown person—and make a lifetime commitment to someone you've just met! In your relationship with your child, you assume a new role that affects almost every part of your life.

During the first five years of life, children change rapidly and dramatically. Parents need to keep readjusting too! When you finally get the baby to sleep through the night, she gives up her morning nap and upsets your routine. You wait for her to crawl, then find her the following week on top of the cupboard. She fusses while getting her teeth, but begins losing them when they've barely been used. Her favorite words change from "Mama" and "Dada" to "No!" Once she's able to, she asks hundreds of questions each day.

You are your child's first and most influential teacher. While learning to be flexible and adaptable to your everchanging child, you are also developing skills to guide and encourage your child as he grows. When he's a baby and you offer comfort when he cries, he begins to learn that he is valued and that people are trustworthy. When he's 2 years old and you remove him, kicking and screaming, from a store, he is learning limits. When he's 5 and you help him make a turn on his bike, he is learning problem-solving skills.

This is what *Parenting Young Children* is all about. Its purpose is to provide:

- a look at the long-term goals of parenting
- information on how young children think, feel, and act
- skills that can increase your enjoyment and effectiveness as a parent
- skills that can develop your child's self-esteem and confidence
- support for yourself as a parent and as a person
- effective ways to teach cooperation and discipline

The principles and skills in *Parenting Young Children* can help you feel more confident in your parenting role. The book suggests a consistent, positive, and democratic approach based on a program called *STEP—Systematic Training for Effective Parenting. Parenting Young Children* applies STEP's principles and methods to the special challenges of parenting infants, toddlers, and preschoolers. This book can be your partner as you work to build healthy patterns of belief and behavior in your young child—patterns that can form the foundation for a lifetime of positive growth.

Yes, parenting young children is a major challenge. But it is a challenge filled with opportunities for both parents and children to experience many joys and satisfactions. With *Parenting Young Children*, you can meet the challenge—and the opportunities—with confidence.

Don Dinkmeyer, Sr.   Don Dinkmeyer, Jr.
Gary D. McKay   Joyce L. McKay
James S. Dinkmeyer

CHAPTER ONE

Understanding Young Children

As a parent of a young child, you are the most important person in your child's life. You want to raise your child to be respectful, self-reliant, happy, healthy, confident, cooperative, and responsible.

You *can* meet the challenge of parenting by:

- learning about how children grow and behave
- becoming skilled at encouraging your child
- discovering ways to listen and talk together
- learning effective, positive ways to discipline

Parenting Young Children can be your guide in meeting this challenge. It has information and skills to help you. You will think about and practice new approaches. As you do this, your skill will grow. Your confidence will too!

The Basics: Special Traits in Each Child

Each child is born with certain qualities, or *traits*. These traits play a part in shaping your child's personality. By recognizing them, you can help your child use these qualities in positive ways.

Here's what you will learn . . .

- Your parenting challenge is to raise a confident, re-spectful, self-reliant, respon-sible, cooperative child.

- Children grow at their own rate and master new skills when they are ready.

- You can help your child develop positive beliefs.

- Play is the "work" of young children.

- Your job is to guide—not to punish or give too much freedom.

Temperament

Temperament means a style of behavior. Some children get hungry and sleepy at regular times. Others are not so regular. Some children easily accept loud noises, bright lights, and new tastes. Others find them upsetting.

Each child's style shows the child's temperament. Understanding this can help you understand your child. It can help you appreciate and work with your child's particular style.

A baby is born with an individual temperament. It stays much the same all through childhood. Temperament has nothing to do with being smart or talented. It refers to the unique qualities a child is born with.

Rate of Development

Children develop at their own rate. They have their own "timetables" for cutting teeth, starting to talk, and being ready for toilet training. These tasks are influenced by a child's *environment* too—by the people, places, and events the child experiences.

Chart 1 at the end of this chapter is helpful. But children can also develop skills at different times.

Luís is 1 year old. He and his dad meet a neighbor in the hall at their apartment. "Is Luís talking yet?" asks Mrs. Robb. "He can say a few words," Luís's dad answers. "Shouldn't he be saying more than that? My little girl knew lots of words at his age!" says Mrs. Robb. "Luís will talk more when he's ready," says Luís's dad.

Parents help children when they *respect* their rates of development. Your job is not to push. Instead, encourage and appreciate your child and offer chances for development. How can you do this?

Think about babies. They need time and space on the floor. This lets them learn to crawl when they are ready. They don't need crawling lessons!

Style of Development

Children's styles develop in their own way. Some children learn and practice new skills in public. Their mistakes don't bother them. Other children wait until they know a skill well. Only then will they show it to other people. Some children babble for months before they say a real word. Others keep quiet until they can put together a simple sentence. Some children's bodies, minds, and feelings develop together. Other children grow in one area at a time.

Children develop at their own rate. You help your child by respecting this rate of development.

Certain kinds of learning come before others. Sitting up and crawling come before walking. Picking up dry cereal comes before printing letters. Playing *beside* other children comes before playing *with* them.

Keep this in mind: Children develop at their own rate. Each child will master a new skill when ready. Knowing that some skills come in order can help you. It lets you know what to get ready for. Then you'll know how to help your child grow.

Babies—Birth to 18 Months Old

In *Parenting Young Children,* we often talk about *babies* or *infants.* What do we mean? Some babies are newborns. Some are sitting up. Some are crawling. Some are just beginning to walk. In general, *babyhood* ends when a child can walk.

Babies are learning to trust adults. They know that someone will:

- feed and dress them
- change their diapers
- listen to their cries
- keep them from danger

Babies are learning to know and trust themselves. They are finding that they can:

- comfort themselves with a thumb or blanket
- get what they want by crawling and grasping

Babies are learning to trust the world around them. They discover that:

- the floor is hard, stuffed animals are soft
- orange food usually tastes good; green food sometimes doesn't
- a warm bath feels good; a shot hurts

Toddlers—18 to 36 Months Old

Toddlers walk—and run—all around. They can be clumsy. This is because they can't control movement like preschoolers can. Toddlers are busy talking too. Their words can be hard to understand.

Toddlers reach for independence. Toddlers know that someone will be there to keep them safe. So they feel freer to push away from parents. Toddlers experiment. They make demands.

Toddlers are learning many things. Each act of independence teaches them about being a person:

- When toddlers insist on doing everything for themselves, they are learning *self-reliance.*
- When they claim all toys are "Mine!" they are learning about *ownership.*
- Toddlers learn about fear and safety when they become afraid of the dark or strangers.
- When they learn to pet the cat gently, toddlers are learning *self-control.*

In these and many other ways, toddlers are taking major steps in growing up.

Preschoolers—3 to 5 Years Old

Preschoolers are older than toddlers. But they are not yet school-aged. They are sure of themselves, their parents, and their caregivers. Now they are ready to plunge into a bigger world of friends and toys.

Preschoolers are creative. They are artists, builders, and inventors. They have great imaginations and start to act out adventures. Preschoolers play "house" and school. They practice adult roles when they:

- feed their dolls and make mud pies for lunch
- ride their trikes as fire engines and build forts from blankets

Preschoolers also create fantasy worlds:

- The bathtub becomes a monster's pool.
- A cardboard box becomes a castle.

Preschoolers beg you to read them stories. They invent their own rhymes, silly words, and stories too. They may decide to shock you with a swearword.

Preschoolers need friends. At this age, children need to learn how people get along. With friends, they "practice" many things: They use ideas, make decisions, settle arguments, and show appreciation.

Beyond the Basics:
You and Your Child's Behavior

You can influence your child in many ways. One way is by thinking about your *expectations*.

The Power of Expectations

Expectations are powerful. Most parents have expectations about parenting. Too often, we expect something negative. We talk about "the terrible twos," "rug rats," or "little monsters."

Young children often sense our expectations and may try to meet them. Think about it: Would life with a 2-year-old be different if we talked about "the terrific twos"? If all we expected was cooperation and good behavior? Keep your expectations positive. Will your child be perfect then? No. But you are likely to get more cooperation.

Stress

Most of us feel a lot of stress. We worry about money and work. We have problems. We don't have enough time for all we want and need to do.

Would life with a 2-year-old be different if we talked about "the terrific twos"?

When people have a lot of stress, they often grow impatient. Parents might argue. They might snap or yell at their children, who then might cry, argue, or worry.

Kavon is 5. His stepsister Nika is 2. Nika grabs Kavon's truck and screams, "Mine!" Kavon tries to pull the truck away. The children start fighting and screaming. Kavon's daddy knows it is best to separate the children quietly. But he feels a lot of stress. He is worried about money. He and his wife are having problems. He made a mistake at work today, and his boss got mad. So he yells at Nika and Kavon. Kavon yells back. Nika throws herself on the floor in a tantrum.

It's easy to let stress get in the way of parenting. But when we do, our children's behavior is likely to get worse, not better. If you feel stressed, step back and take a deep breath. Think about what's important *right now*. Decide *not* to feel so much stress. You can do this! On page 14 is a "Just for You" activity called "Ease the Stress." It shows you a way you can work to calm down when you feel tense.

More "Yes"-Less "No"

Look for ways to say yes instead of no.

Most toddlers start to use the magic word no. Some even say no when they mean yes! Why is no such a popular word with children? Maybe because it's so popular with parents. The wise parent will look for ways to use the word yes more often.

Two-year-old Paul is having a bad morning. He grabs his sister's brand-new birthday gift. His mother says, "No!" He shouts that he wants cookies for breakfast. His mother says, "No!" He demands to play with his toy train. It's time to leave home, so Mother says, "No!"

In a short time, Paul's mother says no three times. But she doesn't have to say it at all. She could take the birthday gift away and give Paul something else to play with. She could ignore his screams for cookies. She could say, "You can play with your train later." Mother might even find a way to say yes. She might say:

- "Yes, you like your sister's present. But it belongs to her. Let's find something you can play with instead."
- "Yes, I like cookies too! But what do we eat for breakfast?"

Paul may keep grumbling. But he will hear his mother's friendly words. Over time, Mother's saying yes may help Paul cooperate more.

Of course, sometimes you will have to say no:

Labels can become self-fulfilling. Work to find positive expectations.

Davisha reached for the knobs on the stove. Her daddy picked her up. He said, "No, Davisha—never touch the stove. It's hot and you might get burned. Here, you can play under the table with these pans." He set Davisha on the floor and gave her some pans and a wooden spoon.

Beliefs and Behavior

Young children are forming *beliefs*. These beliefs come from their experiences:

- Some parents yell or put children down a lot. Then children may begin to believe they are *bad*.

- Some parents say "You can do it!" and "I love you." Then children may begin to believe they are *worthwhile*.

It is possible for children to build positive beliefs about themselves. As a parent, you can influence these beliefs. Positive beliefs lead to positive behavior. You can guide your child to develop positive patterns of behavior. One way to do this is by teaching that feelings are important. Listen to your child's feelings. Respond by showing respect and understanding:

- "It hurts when Kitty scratches."
- "You can hardly wait to get in the bathtub!"

You can also expect respect for your feelings:

- "I don't like biting—it hurts! Let's put you down and give you something else to play with."

This respect shows positive beliefs. It shows that you accept your child's feelings and that you have feelings too. It shows positive ways to talk about feelings.

Young children are self-centered. This is natural. Yet, from the beginning, you can show respect for feelings. Your child will see and feel this respect. Slowly, your child will learn to respect other people's feelings too.

Think of this as a plant that grows with each positive influence: Positive beliefs lead to positive behavior. The positive behavior builds more positive beliefs that bring about more positive behavior. Now is the time to begin guiding your child—to start the positive cycle.

Important People in Your Child's Life

Your child is young. In the lives of young children, mothers and fathers, brothers and sisters are the most important people of all. If you are married, you and your spouse can share equally in the job of parenting. Your child will see that married people help each other. With your partner's support, you will find it easier to stay calm and respectful.

You may be a single parent. If you are, do the best you can to share the job of parenting with your child's other parent. That is the ideal situation for children. Of course, it isn't always possible. Then you may want to find another adult of the opposite sex to spend some time with your child. The person should be someone you know and trust.

Grandparents often give this kind of support to their grown children. A child who has a grandpa or grandma is lucky. Their relationship can be special.

Jonah is 4 years old. His mom, Dawn, goes to school two nights a week. On those nights, Jonah goes to his "grampa's" apartment. He and Grampa have a special time. Grampa reads to Jonah. He tells stories about when Jonah's mom was a little girl. Together, they build towns made of blocks. Jonah likes to sit at the kitchen table and draw pictures. Sometimes Grampa makes Jonah's favorite soup.

Dawn needs her father's help. And she is glad that Jonah and his Grampa can have time together. It's hard for Dawn as a single parent. She has learned to ask for her father's advice. Her father has learned to give it only when Dawn asks. This didn't happen naturally. Dawn and her father worked hard to figure out how to do what's best for the family.

Working out an adult relationship may be hard. But it is important. And it's worth the effort. One reward is your child's special friendship with a grandparent. Another is the support you will have as a parent. A third is the new closeness you might find in this adult relationship.

Play is children's "work."

The Power of Play

Early in life, children move into the world of play. Play is another important area in which you can help your child grow.

Play is something adults do as a change from work. For children, play *is* their "work." Children must play to develop. In play, they learn about the world and their place in it. They practice the skills they will need as they grow. Through trial and error while playing, they learn about life.

Play With Your Child

Infants, toddlers, and preschoolers can enjoy playing with parents in many ways. Playing together helps build a positive relationship. It helps children learn.

When children are punished for "being bad," they may learn to fear parents.

Mali is 8 months old. Her mother spends some time each evening playing with her. Mali loves to play pat-a-cake. She is learning to copy the sounds and movements her mother makes.

Drew is 2 years old. After his nap, he loves to play peek-a-boo with his dad. Dad hides his own face behind a blanket. Then he lowers the blanket, a bit at a time, to peek at Drew. Drew reaches up to grab Dad's nose. It's suddenly covered again with the blanket! Drew giggles. Then Dad covers Drew's face for a quick second, and the game begins again. Drew is learning a fun game that he can follow. And, without words, he's learning about taking turns.

Some older children invent playmates. These make-believe friends let children use their imaginations and practice social skills.

Four-year-old Steffie drapes an old towel around her shoulders and becomes a superhero. She wants help with her super adventures. So she imagines a friend named Max. Sometimes Steffie shows Max her toys. Sometimes she and Max play together with her stuffed animals.

Children need opportunities to play without their parents too. This gives them freedom to explore and learn. It's also important for you to play with your child. If your child wants you to, join in. Enjoy this chance to have fun together! You can also teach your child a skill through play. Or you can help your child express feelings. Using a puppet or stuffed animal to "talk" can help a child put feelings into words.

Choose Toys Carefully

Toys can help develop children's imagination and skills. Look for toys for your child that are:

- **safe**—fire-resistant, with no sharp edges or small parts that could be swallowed

- **sturdy**—so they won't break easily

- **simple**—so children can be creative in using them (for example, blocks, sand, and art materials)

- **age-appropriate**—geared to the child's age, ability, and development

Start Early to Set a Parenting Plan

Often, actions speak louder than words. You want your child to grow up to be self-reliant, respectful, self-confident, responsible, and cooperative. A carefully chosen parenting approach, or style, can guide you as you make decisions about day-to-day problems and challenges.

There are many styles of parenting. The three that are most common are *giving orders*, *giving in*, and *giving choices*.

Giving Orders

This style of parenting is often called *authoritarian*. The parents are strict. They set a lot of rules. The children are expected to obey the rules exactly. Often strict parents reward and punish children to keep them in line.

What Do Children Learn?

Rewards lead children to expect payment for "being good." When children are punished for "being bad," they may learn to fear and resent parents. Children need freedom to grow and learn. They also need the chance to make choices. This lets them learn limits and responsibility.

Giving In

Giving in is also called *permissive* parenting. Permissive parents set no limits. Children grow up without guidelines. The parents give in to whatever the children may want. We often say that these children are "spoiled."

What Do Children Learn?

Without limits, children will have trouble getting along with others. These children usually learn to do as they please. They *don't* learn to care about the feelings and rights of others. Society sets limits. Children with no limits on their behavior will have difficulty learning how to behave in society.

Giving Choices

What approach to parenting will help you reach your goal? We think the *democratic* method of giving choices is the most effective.

Democratic parenting is based on equality and respect. We all have different abilities, responsibilities, and experiences. But we are still equally worthwhile as humans.

Does this mean that your child has the same privileges as you do? No. It means that you recognize the importance of your child's wishes. It also means that you involve your child in decision making when appropriate. Democratic parents give a child choices that fit the child's age and development.

Encouragement
STEP

Make an effort to understand your child. Ask yourself:

- **What is my child feeling?**
- **What does my child seem to believe?**

Respond so your child knows you understand. Be careful not to judge or criticize. Practice responding to these statements:

- **"I can't do it!"**
- **"You're mean."**
- **"You like Sara more than me!"**
- **"Kai's mommy doesn't like me!"**

Chapter 3 deals with encouragement. Each chapter of this book has an "Encouragement STEP." These "steps" will help you get into the encouragement habit!

Young children's ability to make choices is limited. They can't yet depend on themselves to keep the rules. They need adults to set the limits for them.

Ahmed is 2 years old. His grandma can't expect him to ignore a plate of cookies. He depends on her to put the cookies out of his reach.

When children go past the limits, they need parents to follow through with *consequences.*

Maria is 5 years old. She often leaves toys and books all over. Her papa talks to her quietly. He tells her that she is old enough to be responsible for picking things up. Papa gives Maria a choice: She may put each thing away when she is through with it. Or Papa will pick up the things and put them away until he thinks Maria is ready to be responsible for them. After missing a few of her things for a day or two, Maria will learn to pick up her things.

The democratic method helps children become responsible. It does this by giving choices within set limits.

What Do Children Learn?

A democratic parenting style gives young children freedom within limits. Children learn that their choices count and carry responsibility. They learn respect.

In the coming chapters, you will explore many ways to guide your child. They are based on your own understanding, example, and skills. From this base, you can begin to develop courage and cooperation.

Young children need parents to set limits for them.

THIS WEEK

Look at your expectations for your child.

- Are they positive? negative?
- What changes would you like to make in your expectations?

POINTS TO REMEMBER

1. The challenge of parenting is to raise a child who is happy, respectful, self-reliant, healthy, confident, cooperative, and responsible.

2. Each child is born with an individual temperament. Accept your child's temperament and build on it.

3. Each child goes through stages of development at his or her own rate and style.

4. Children master new skills when they are ready.
   - Babies learn to trust adults, themselves, and the world around them.
   - Toddlers try independence.
   - Preschoolers create their own worlds. They play with language. They practice adult roles and learn to get along with other children.

5. Parents have expectations. Children sense parents' expectations and often act as expected.

6. Easing stress can help you be a more effective parent.

7. Find and create opportunities to say yes rather than no.

8. Positive beliefs will lead to positive behavior patterns. You encourage positive beliefs when you show and teach respect and love.

9. Other adults can support you in your job as a parent.

10. Give children time to play. Play is their "work," and they must do it to develop and grow.

11. Help your child cooperate and be responsible by setting limits and giving choices.

JUST FOR YOU

Ease the Stress

Being a parent is a big job. If you didn't feel stress sometimes, you wouldn't be human! Stress is a response to upsetting events. It can be something physical: a headache, high blood pressure, a racing heart. It can be emotional: You might feel worried or have trouble sleeping.

What can you do to ease and handle stress? Here are a few ideas:

1. **Use deep breathing.** Breathe deeply for fifteen seconds. Let your breathing pace itself. Say "calm" as you breathe in. Say "down" as you breathe out. "Calm . . . down. . . ."

2. **Use self-talk.** Say simple, upbeat things to yourself: "Take it easy." "You're okay." "This will pass."

3. **Be prepared.** If you think something is going to be stressful, be ready for it. Take a few deep breaths. Talk to yourself before facing the situation.

4. **Take a new look.** Think of a difficult situation as a challenge—not as something that you can't handle. See it as a chance to find new strength in yourself.

5. **Pat yourself on the back.** Accept yourself. Take time every day to think about your good qualities. Tell yourself: "I'm capable." "I'm worthwhile." "I make my own decisions." Encourage yourself.

6. **Keep a journal.** Write about stressful situations. Note what you did to help yourself ease the stress. Write yourself notes about how well you are doing.

Chart 1

DEVELOPMENT: BIRTH TO AGE 5

Every child may not match the chart. A child develops a skill when he or she is ready.

Age	What Child Learns	What Child Does
Birth–3 months	Trust, cooperation, personal power (such as effects of crying)	Gains head control; grasps and holds; makes sounds. Smiles in response to others. Shows distress, delight, excitement, boredom. Is forming routine for eating, sleeping.
3–6 months	To affect the environment through body movement	Sits with support. Reaches; grabs objects suddenly. Imitates sounds; uses sounds to show likes, dislikes. Recognizes familiar objects. Is very social.
6–9 months	More awareness of consequences of behavior	Sits up, stands with help, crawls. Uses thumb and fingers to grasp small items. Drinks from cup. Is growing more independent. Imitates behavior. May say "Mama" and "Dada." May recognize own name and word "no." Notices others' feelings—joins other children if they cry, laugh. Is anxious about strangers; may be fearful, even of what is familiar.
9–12 months	More awareness of consequences of behavior	May crawl up and down stairs. Stands. Is better at grasping, holding. Often cooperates in getting dressed. May say a few words. Shows and recognizes moods. Is aware of unspoken communication. Is often loving; is more assertive. Fears strangers, being separated from parent.
1–2 years	Beginnings of self-confidence	Walks (usually by fifteen months). Explores; empties, fills things; drops, throws things. Feeds self. Wants to be both independent, dependent. Uses clearer language. Becomes a toddler.

Age	What Child Learns	What Child Does
2–3 years	More self-confidence	Grows more independent—wants to do things own way. At times, wants to return to babyhood. Moves around without bumping into things. Speaks in sentences of 2–4 words. Asks "what?" and "why?" Has longer attention span, memory. Likes to help. Plays beside other children. Gets greater bowel and bladder control.
3–4 years	More sociability	Cooperates more. Improves in coordination. Is talkative; enjoys hearing stories. Wants to be like parents. Recognizes sex differences. Chooses clothes; dresses self. Likes to be with same-age children. Learns to take turns, share. Begins to understand ideas of *yesterday, today, tomorrow.*
4–5 years	To grow in abilities already learned	Prefers children over adults. Has make-believe friends. Has firm sense of home, family. Is very active—runs, jumps, climbs. Is increasing fine-motor abilities. Likes to talk, express ideas, ask complex questions. Likely to have good bladder, bowel control; may have accidents. Is growing in awareness of time.
5–6 years	To adapt to the world of childhood and to be ready for school	Begins to care about other children's opinions. Has more advanced reasoning powers. Has good control of hands, legs; eye-hand coordination not fully developed—has accidents involving hands. Becomes right or left handed. Is talkative, has good vocabulary. Is loving, helpful to parents. Likes to make friends. Plays with both sexes. Develops sense of fairness. Wants to be independent, treated like an adult.

CHAPTER TWO

Understanding
Young Children's
Behavior

Keang and Tessa are 4 years old. The dentist visits their preschool. She scrubs giant teeth with a big toothbrush. Then she asks, "Who will sit on this stool and let me floss their teeth?" Keang shouts, "I will! I will!" The dentist flosses his teeth. She explains to the other children what she is doing. Keang is so happy, he can hardly sit still. Tessa watches quietly. She holds her hands to her mouth and copies what the dentist does.

Tessa and Keang have different personalities. Keang is outgoing and ready to do new things. He is happy when he's being noticed. Tessa is less outgoing and very watchful. She practices what she sees.

Where Do My Child's Beliefs Come From?

Like all people, children need to belong—to feel they are accepted. Children have *beliefs* about what to do to belong.

Children form their most basic beliefs by the time they are 6. Each child learns to fit into groups—family, friends, school. They may be like Tessa—watching and quietly trying new things. Or, like Keang, they may rush into things full of excitement. Both Tessa and Keang believe that the world is friendly and find their place by cooperation. But they show their belief in different ways.

Other children may have different views. Some may believe the world is unfriendly. These children may avoid being with other people.

Here's what you will learn . . .

- Your child has beliefs about how to belong.

- Your child's behavior comes from these beliefs.

- Not all troublesome behavior is misbehavior.

- Children's misbehavior has one of four goals: attention, power, revenge, or displaying inadequacy.

- Focusing on the positive encourages positive behavior.

Starting at birth, each child learns a special way to belong.

Marco's father always told his son, "You're too little! You'll get hurt! Please be careful!" Marco decided, "The world is a scary place. I can't trust myself." This belief made sense to Marco. It fit with his experience. But in the real world, it wasn't logical.

Children are not aware of their beliefs. This is true for adults too. But our beliefs are like a map we follow to decide how to fit in, resist, or stay neutral.

Beliefs come from each child's view of four things:

- what is important in the family
- what the parents say and do
- the style of parenting
- the child's place in the family

What Is Important in the Family

Every family has a unique mood or tone. We call this the *family atmosphere.* Also, adults in every family have values. The combination of atmosphere and values gives the child a message about what is important in a family.

For children with two parents, a family value is something that's important to *both* parents. This is true even if the parents don't agree about it.

Esther and Tyrone have two children: Keesha is 2 and Shantelle is 3. They are raising their children to be active. Esther likes competing at sports. When she plays, she wants to win. Tyrone enjoys exercise for the fun of it. He likes to jog or ride a bike on his own.

Sports is a value for this family. As Keesha and Shantelle grow older, they may choose to compete in sports like soccer or basketball. Or they may choose individual sports. One of the girls may love sports. The other may reject sports. Both girls will choose how they respond to this family value.

Changes in the family affect the family atmosphere:

- A single parent marries. The new husband or wife brings new family values.

- Parents get separated or divorced. Children become more aware of family values—especially those that parents don't agree on.

- A parent forms a new relationship or remarries. Children often become part of two families with two different family atmospheres and values.

Children learn from the important adults in their lives. They learn what being a woman or a man means. They also learn about relationships. Children learn how adults treat each other. They watch and may copy what adults say and do.

By your actions and words, you show your child what is important to you. You help your child begin to learn what being an adult means. When parents respect and value their children, themselves, their spouse, and others, their children learn about respect.

Parenting Styles

In Chapter 1 you read about parenting styles. A parent's style influences what children believe:

- **When parents shout orders or demand changes, some children may resist and compete. They may believe that being the boss is the way to belong.**
- **When parents give choices, children often learn that cooperation is a way people can live together. They see that every person is important.**

The Child's Place in the Family

The child's "place" in the family is called *birth order*. It affects the child's beliefs. A child may be an only child, the oldest, the second, the middle, or the youngest—the "baby."

An Only Child

Only children are used to being the center of attention. Sometimes they have trouble getting along with other children. Many only children spend a lot of time playing alone. Then they learn ways to entertain themselves. Often, too, only children spend time with their parents and their parents' friends. They can be creative and often act grown-up.

An Oldest Child

An oldest child was once an only child. Giving up all the attention can be hard for an oldest child. Often, an oldest child wants to be the boss. As they grow, many oldest children learn to lead and to cooperate. They often learn responsibility because their parents and the younger children may look to them for help.

You teach mutual respect when you respect and value your child, yourself, and others.

A Second Child

A second child never has the parent's full attention the way a first child once did. Second children may work hard to keep up with or overtake an older sister or brother. Sometimes a second child decides to be the opposite of the oldest child. If the oldest child is usually "good," the second may become "bad." If the oldest child is a loner, the second may become the sociable one.

A Middle Child

A middle child often feels "squeezed" between the older and younger children. Middle children may learn ways to get along with all kinds of people. Some middle children are not sure of themselves. They want life to be fair. They may misbehave to get attention. They often can adapt themselves easily to new situations.

A Youngest Child

Youngest children usually don't have to do as much for themselves as older ones. They may feel safe and become charming and friendly. Or they may feel left out and be bossy and demanding. Some younger children give up because they can't yet do what older children can do. Some may use their charm to get help from other people. Youngest children sometimes work hard to be as skillful as their brothers and sisters.

What Does the Child See?

A "place" in the family isn't based only on actual birth order. It is based on how the child sees *his or her place.*

The children in one family are Elena (12), Tomás (4), and Alfonso (2). In birth order, Elena is the oldest. But she was an only child for eight years. Even though she has brothers, Elena acts more like an only child. Tomás is the middle child in birth order. But he is more aware of Alfonso than Elena. Tomás acts more like the older child of two.

The Child's Place Changes

As new children come into a family, each child's place changes. For example, a single parent may marry someone with children. Each child has a new place in the new family. But children don't forget their place in the first family. That role plays an important part as they make changes.

Children sometimes compete for their place in the family. For example, a firstborn may struggle to keep the place of an "only" child. This competition greatly affects beliefs and behavior. When children compete, one child succeeds. Another becomes discouraged or fails.

Birth-Order Beliefs: What You Can Do

To help your child form positive beliefs about birth order:

- Avoid calling the youngest child "the baby."
- Ask the youngest child to be a helper.
- Don't always talk about the oldest child first.
- Oldest and only children need to learn give-and-take with other children. To help them learn, place them in child care or pre-school.
- Don't give your middle child too much pity or sympathy.
- Plan time to do things with each child individually.

Why Do Children Behave as They Do?

At the same time children are forming beliefs, they are forming *patterns of behavior.* Children use certain behaviors because they work to reach the goal of fitting in.

Early childhood is a time of learning how to belong. As young children grow, they find that certain responses from parents give them a feeling of belonging. They learn ways to act to get those responses.

Jason is 2 1/2 years old. He wants to belong by helping his dad wash the car. Jason takes the sponge from the bucket of water. He slaps it on the side of the car. As he does, he smiles and says, "I wash the car with Daddy." Dad tells his son, "Thanks for your help, Jason. You're getting the car good and clean." Jason starts to see himself as a helpful person.

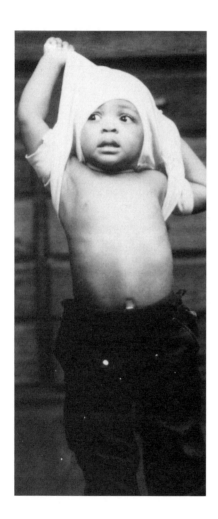

Jason's dad is helping him learn a positive way to belong. At another time, Dad might not have time to give Jason what he wants. He might say, "You're too little to help. Go and play." Jason will still be trying to belong. He might cry or grab the hose and squirt his dad and the car. His dad will have to deal with the negative behavior. Jason will have found a way to get his dad involved with him. That, too, is a way to belong. What will happen the next time Jason wants to feel included? He may remember that he can use negative behavior to win a "place" with his dad.

Psychiatrist Rudolf Dreikurs found that when children misbehave, they are *discouraged*. They want to belong. But they do not believe they can belong in useful ways. They find that misbehavior pays off. It helps them feel that they belong.

When children misbehave, they want something. They may want:

- to get attention
- to have power
- to get revenge
- to display inadequacy

Dreikurs called these the four goals of misbehavior. Understanding these goals is important. Doing so can help you know what your child believes and wants. This can help you decide how to guide your child to more positive behavior.

What Is "Misbehavior"?

Dreikurs gave the word *misbehavior* a special meaning. He was talking about behavior that comes from *failing to find a place through cooperation*. But not everything we commonly call misbehavior fits this definition. To decide if a child is "misbehaving," look at developmental stages.

Ari is 9 months old. When he pulls the cat's tail, he doesn't want power. He is just curious. Curiosity is normal in a child this age.

Bridget, who is 14 months old, dives for the dirt in a potted plant. She doesn't want attention. She just wants to feel the dirt.

Yoko, age 2, screams and runs around at a party. She has become overexcited.

At times, children use negative behavior because they are curious, tired, sick, hungry, or bored. They might be clumsy. They might be trying to help. We may find this behavior troublesome. But it is *not really misbehavior.* At times, when we think our children should just "shape up," we may have unrealistic expectations.

Three-year-old Maruf ties a rope around his dog's neck. He drags the dog for a "walk" behind his trike. Maruf just wants to share his fun with his pet.

Naomi, who is 5, crosses the busy street by her aunt's home without asking permission. Her aunt is horrified. But Naomi lives on a quiet street. She is allowed to cross it without asking. No one told her the rules were different at her aunt's.

At times, your child may "misbehave" without meaning to. How you react can influence what the child does next time. You can learn to react in ways that help your child find a better way to behave.

Pete is a toddler. He spilled his milk. It may have been an accident. Or he may have wanted to see how milk looks falling to the floor. Either way, Pete's mom will react. She might yell, "Pete—don't do that! Look at the mess you made!" Then Pete may "spill" milk again when he wants his mom's attention. The behavior will become <u>mis</u>behavior.

But Mom might give a more low-key response. She might bring a sponge to Pete and say, "Oops, looks like the milk spilled. We'd better clean it up. Here, Pete, you can mop the tray." In this way, Mom will build Pete's belief that mistakes are okay. He will see that he can help put things right.

To see a change in your child's behavior, change your own behavior first.

The Goals of Misbehavior

Let's look at the four goals of misbehavior. They can help us tell the difference between troublesome but normal behavior and true misbehavior.

Attention. All children need attention. Giving a baby or young child attention is a big part of a parent's job.

Four-year-old Patti learns a new trick on the jungle gym. She calls to her mom to watch. She wants appropriate attention. Mom is sitting on a bench reading. She looks up to watch and says, "Look what you can do by yourself! I'm glad you're having fun." Mom goes back to her reading. Patti plays and practices her skills.

Patti has asked for, and gotten, helpful attention. She feels she belongs. Mom has recognized Patti's accomplishment. Mom has seen how much Patti enjoys climbing.

When does attention become a goal of misbehavior? When children believe they can belong *only* by demanding and getting attention.

What if Patti said, "Look at my new trick . . . Now look again . . . Do you like it? Watch my other tricks. Did you see that? Watch me do it again! . . . Mommy—watch!" If Mom tried to read, Patti might go on with her bids for attention. She might even fall off the jungle gym. Then she would have a <u>big</u> dose of attention. Mom would know that Patti believed she belonged <u>only</u> by getting her mother's attention.

Power. A positive sense of power gives children a feeling of control. It is an important step toward independence.

Darryl, 18 months old, wants to feed himself. His parents give him a child-sized plate and spoon. They accept that things are messier because he feeds himself. Sometimes they say to Darryl: "Look what you can do! You're feeding yourself!" Darryl is using power in a good way. He is learning to belong in positive ways. His parents' reaction supports this.

What might happen if Darryl's parents insist on feeding him?

Darryl might feel frustrated about not being able to feed himself. He might refuse to eat. Or he might demand his favorite bib. Maybe Darryl would insist on eating while standing up. He might throw his food across the room as a way to say, "I'm the boss!" If his parents give in or fight, Darryl would push for more power. He would believe he belonged by being the one in charge.

Revenge. If children lose a power struggle, they may choose the third goal of misbehavior—revenge. When children seek revenge, they believe they can belong *only* by hurting others as they have been hurt. They want to get even.

Megan is 4. Every workday morning, her father takes her to day care. He wants Megan to get as much sleep as possible. So he waits to wake her until the last minute. He has to dress her quickly.

Positive power gives children a feeling of control. Parents need to know how to share power

How we react may determine whether the behavior will be repeated as a way of achieving one of the four goals of misbehavior.

Megan asks for attention by playing "Catch me if you can." Dad chases her. He feels annoyed and resentful. The negative attention invites Megan to take power. She kicks and screams as her father tries to put her jacket on. A full-scale power struggle begins. Megan hollers, "I won't!" Dad shouts, "Oh, yes you will!" He forces Megan into her clothes. She screams, "I hate you! You're mean!" They both feel hurt and angry as they go to day care.

The goal of revenge is rare before the preschool years. At times, a toddler *might* seek revenge. Babies do not misbehave to get revenge. The toddler and preschool years are when children first move into misbehaving for revenge.

Displaying inadequacy. Infants usually do not display inadequacy. In most cases, toddlers don't either. This is because a child who displays inadequacy is very discouraged. The discouragement takes place over time. It comes from months or years of not finding a way to belong through positive behavior. Children with this goal have come to believe they belong only by convincing others that they are helpless. They give up. They also convince those around them to give up on them.

A child who displays inadequacy is very discouraged. It's important to encourage such a child.

Bobby is 5. His uncle sees him coloring. "Have you learned to write your name yet, Bobby?" he asks. "No," says Bobby. "Here," says his uncle. "Let me show you how." "No," answers Bobby. "I can't do it." Bobby hangs his head. "Well," says his uncle, "what are you coloring?"

Bobby's uncle has changed his focus to something Bobby feels comfortable doing. This is encouraging. It can be the first step toward helping Bobby believe he can write.

But why is Bobby discouraged about writing his name?

When he was 4, Bobby began learning to print the letters. He turned some of them around, like this: *Boddy*. Many young children do this. His father would say, "No, Bobby. That's not right. Those are *d*'s, not *b*'s." Over time, Bobby grew discouraged about writing his name. Now he has given up.

Bobby's father was trying to help. But he didn't allow mistakes to happen. Mistakes are part of learning! What if he had changed his expectations? He could have ignored the backward letters. He could have said to Bobby, "Look at how you're learning to write your name! Is it fun?"

How Can I Tell If My Child Is Misbehaving?

Infants usually don't misbehave. You can assume the infant is not misbehaving.

A cranky, crying baby may be telling you that she is hungry or tired. She may need some gentle rocking before she can fall asleep.

It is *possible* that an older baby may begin to misbehave for power and attention. But during the first year of life, the child more likely is simply trying to have real needs met. What if you believe your child's needs are being met, but troublesome behavior continues? Then your baby *might* be starting to pursue attention or power as a goal of misbehavior. In this case, wait a few minutes to respond to the cries. This may help tell you what is wrong.

Look for Clues

As your child gets older, you will find recognizing true misbehavior easier. How can you identify the goal? Look for your own response to the behavior.

Identifying the Goal

Look at three things:

1. **how you feel when the misbehavior happens**
2. **what you do about the misbehavior**
3. **how your child responds to what you do**

Attention

If your child demands attention:

1. **You will probably *feel annoyed*.**
2. **You'll *remind or coax*.**
3. **Your child may *stop the misbehavior*—for now. Later, the child *may repeat the act or do something else* for more attention.**

Power

If your child wants to show power:

1. **You may *feel angry*.**
2. **You may *try to make the child do what you want*. Or you might *give in*.**
3. **If you fight, the child will *fight back*. If you give in, the child will *stop misbehaving*—having gotten what was wanted.**

Revenge

If your child feels hurt and wants revenge:

1. **You might feel *hurt and angry*.**
2. **You may *try to get even*.**
3. **The child *seeks more revenge*. You have a "war" of revenge on your hands.**

Remember, babies do not pursue the goal of revenge. Toddlers may seek revenge at times. But their behavior can be out of bounds because they are upset or overexcited.

Displaying Inadequacy

If your child displays inadequacy:

1. **You will most likely *feel like giving up*. You agree that the child is helpless.**
2. **You *take no action* because you have given up. You may *tell the child you agree that the task is too hard*.**
3. **The child *does not improve*.**

Watch for "Passive" Goals

Displaying inadequacy is *passive* behavior—the child does nothing. The other three goals may sometimes involve passive behavior too:

* A child may expect to be waited on. The child may be passively seeking attention.

Infants usually don't misbehave, You can assume the infant is <u>not</u> misbehaving

- A child silently refuses to budge. The child may be showing passive power.
- A child may give you hateful stares. This can be a passive form of revenge.

You identify these passive goals in the same way: Check your feelings, the action you take, and your child's response to that action.

More About Misbehavior Goals

You've learned that your child needs to belong. Misbehavior is one way your child seeks to do this. This doesn't mean your child thinks, "I want power" or "I want to get even." Rather, children discover that misbehavior works for them—it gives them a payoff. They know this by how parents respond.

Children aren't usually aware of the goals of their misbehavior. They may also misbehave for more than one goal. This will depend on how they see a situation.

Mario is 3. At home, he clowns around to get attention. This helps him belong. But at preschool, Mario's clowning doesn't get him the attention he wants. So he starts to demand attention in other ways. He follows the teacher around and interrupts her when she's with another child. He pushes to be first in line. At school, Mario's search for attention is becoming a power struggle.

In the same way, one type of behavior can be used for different goals.

One 5 year old who can tie her own shoes may wait for her parent to tie them. She's seeking attention. Another 5 year old who can also tie his shoes may not be seeking attention. He may really believe he can't do it. He is displaying inadequacy.

Different behavior can also be used to achieve the same goal.

Two-year-old Clara doesn't want to get into the car. She shows her power by crying. Later she doesn't want to go to bed. She shows her power by refusing to go.

Remember that you can find the goal of misbehavior by how you feel, what you do, and how your child responds to what you do.

What Can I Do When My Child Misbehaves?

Do parents cause children to misbehave? No. Our children choose the way they behave. However, the way we respond *influences* the child's behavior.

Give positive attention when your child is not expecting it.

If we respond as our children expect, they are on the way to reaching their negative goals. Our responses help them get there. Children won't stop a behavior that works. If whining gets attention, why stop? Even "Stop whining" is better for some children than no attention.

But if we respond in some other way, we send a different message. Our words and actions let them know that we won't support their misbehavior. In this way, over time, we can help them choose positive goals and behavior.

Decide ahead of time how you will respond to a certain behavior. Remember, too, to encourage any positive movement. Keep in mind that changes won't happen immediately.

Attention. When possible, ignore misbehavior that seeks attention. Choose not to be annoyed, Avoid always giving attention when the child is asking for it. Be sure to give positive attention when your child is not expecting it. Positive attention builds the child's feeling of being valued and accepted.

Three-year-old Bryna often seeks attention by making noise while her mom and stepfather, Derek, watch the news. They have learned to ignore Bryna's noise. When necessary, they remove Bryna to her room to play by herself during this half hour.

Bryna's mother and stepdad also make a point of noticing Bryna at times when she isn't seeking attention.

One night Bryna's mother saw her husband reading the paper. Bryna was curled up beside him paging through a picture book. Her mother said, "Bryna, it's so nice to see you reading quietly next to Derek." Later that evening. Mother said to Bryna, "Why don't you get that book you were looking at? We can read it together now." Bryna is learning that she deserves and will receive attention, but not on demand!

Power. Refuse to fight or give in—don't let yourself become angry. If possible, let your child experience the *consequences*—the results—of the misbehavior.

Two-year-old Todd refused to eat his lunch. His dad used to argue and try to trick him. Finally, Dad tried to force Todd to eat by keeping him in his high chair. Lately, Dad is trying a new approach. He gives Todd a small morning snack and a healthy lunch. If Todd does not decide to eat after several minutes, Dad simply lifts him down from the high chair. "I guess you're not hungry," he says. "Maybe you'll feel more like eating at suppertime." Dad offers only juice for Todd's afternoon snack. At supper, he provides a balanced meal. Todd sees that refusing to eat won't start a power struggle anymore. Instead, he has to live with the consequences of not eating.

Your child can't have a battle for power or revenge if you refuse to fight or get even.

Revenge. Changing a cycle of revenge isn't easy. It takes time. But your child can't have a battle of revenge if you won't join in. When your child is after revenge, refuse to feel hurt. Instead of trying to get even, work to build trust and mutual respect.

The parents of 4-year-old Emily are separated. Lately, at bedtime, Emily says, "No! I don't want you—I want Daddy!" Mother feels hurt. But she knows acting hurt or angry won't help Emily cope. So Mother stays calm. She tells Emily, "I know you miss Daddy. When you visit him this weekend, he can put you to bed." Mother stays respectful. She lets Emily know that she understands Emily's feelings. Over time, this will help Emily learn that she doesn't have to misbehave to deal with her feelings.

Displaying inadequacy. A child who displays inadequacy is very discouraged. Do not give up on such a child! Avoid criticism. Find any area of strength to encourage. Focus on the child's slightest effort or improvement.

Kwami is 5. He believes he can't learn to ride a bike. His friends ride bikes at the park. Kwami sits on the swing by himself. His grandma says nothing about riding. Instead, she looks for things Kwami does well. She says, "You really know how to pump high on the swing, Kwami! Can you show me how?" Over time, this kind of encouragement can help Kwami. He can see that he can do many things. Later, this may help him find the courage to try to ride a bike. Patience and encouragement will go a long way toward helping Kwami build confidence in himself.

The Flip Side: Positive Behavior Goals

You have seen that children's beliefs can lead to misbehavior. Each belief that leads to misbehavior has a "flip side"—a positive belief that can lead to better behavior goals.

Involvement. A child who wants attention sends this message: "I want to be part of things. Please help me learn to contribute." Encourage your child to help and join in. This helps refocus the goal of attention. Imagine your child saying, "Catch me being good."

Independence. Positive power means being responsible for one's own behavior and choices. The child might be saying: "Please give me choices so I can learn to be responsible and independent." Instead of having power struggles, look for ways to give your child these choices. This helps your child to believe "I can use my power in a helpful way."

Encouragement
STEP

This week, make a special effort to show acceptance of your child. Notice how this can help build your child's self-confidence.

Be aware of times you want to judge or criticize. Find a way to show support instead. For example, you might say:

- "You were mad, and you used words instead of hitting. I'm glad you remembered."

- "It's hard to wait for your friend to come. Thanks for being so patient."

Fairness. Children who seek revenge often want fairness. Their message is:"I want things to be fair, Please help me learn to cooper-ate." Guiding your child to play and share equally encourages this.

Being capable. In displaying inadequacy, your child's message might be: "I need time to think by myself. I want to succeed. Please help me learn to trust myself." Work to build your child's positive feelings about herself or himself. Point out what the child can do, Imagine your child saying, "No matter what I say or do, don't ever give up on me."

In the next few chapters, you will learn many ways to talk and listen to your child. You'll look at how to help your child form posi-tive beliefs and find positive ways to belong.

THIS WEEK

Observe your child's behavior.

- Is the behavior due to the child's level of development or expe-rience?

- Is the behavior really *mis*behavior? If so, ask yourself:

  1. What did my child do?
  2. How did I feel?
  3. What did I do about it?
  4. What did my child do then?
  5. What do I think the goal of misbehavior was?

Consider how you might change your response and begin to redi-rect the misbehavior. Also, look for opportunities to help your child develop positive goals.

POINTS TO REMEMBER

1. Beliefs come from a child's view of what is important in the family, what the parents say and do, the style of parenting, and the child's place.

2. All children want to belong, Beliefs affect how a child decides to belong.

3. Children get a feeling of belonging through both useful behavior and misbehavior.

4. Sometimes we expect too much. Children might be curious, tired, sick, hungry, or bored. Then their behavior may trouble us. This is not always misbehavior.

5. There are four goals of misbehavior:
   - attention
   - power
   - revenge
   - display of inadequacy

6. To identify a child's goal, look at:
   - how you feel when your child misbehaves
   - what you do about it
   - how your child responds to what you do

7. Recognize that an infant is usually not misbehaving but has a specific need.

8. Infants do not misbehave for revenge or to display inadequacy. Toddlers rarely display inadequacy.

9. When your child misbehaves, do or say something your child does not expect. Give positive attention and recognition; work to build trust and self-confidence.

JUST FOR YOU

What's Your Priority?

We all need to belong. How we do this depends on our *priorities*—those things that are most important to us. One set of priorities has to do with how we relate to other people.

To find your own priorities, take this simple test. Which of the following ideas is most important to you? Put a "1" next to it. Put a "2" by the next most important. Rank the others "3" and "4".

_____ A.   I want to avoid being rejected.

_____ B.   I want to avoid being embarrassed.

_____ C.   I want to avoid stress or conflict.

_____ D.   I want to avoid being unproductive.

A. If you ranked this choice first, *pleasing* is probably your highest priority. You want to be liked by other people.

B. If you ranked this choice first, *control* is probably your highest priority. You want to be in charge. You don't want to be controlled by someone else.

C. If you ranked this choice first, *comfort* is probably your highest priority. You don't want to be disturbed by stress or conflict.

D. If you ranked this choice first, *excellence* is probably your highest priority. You want to have meaning in your life.

The following chart lists some of the ways the different priorities can affect you and your children.

Priority	Pluses for you	Minuses for you	Pluses for Your Child	Minuses for Your Child
Pleasing	You may get along with others. You may know what people want.	You may feel (and be) taken advantage of, disrespected.	May experience less conflict, may feel easily understood.	May be disrespectful, take advantage of others.
Control	You may be logical and organized.	You may find it hard to get close to people to share feelings.	May learn limits and organization.	May face power contests, be afraid to share feelings.
Comfort	You may be easygoing and have few conflicts.	You may feel unfulfilled, a lack of accomplishment.	May experience has conflict, feel able to purse own interests.	Interests may go unrecognized, seem unimportant.
Excellence	You may be capable and creative.	You may feel overburdened, overresponsible.	May be creative, have positive outlook on life.	May feel inadequate, need to be perfect.

- What positive effects does your priority have on your life? on your approach to parenting?
- What negative effects does it have?
- What changes might you want to make?

Chart 2
GOALS OF MISBEHAVIOR

BABIES

- The concept of goals usually doesn't apply to infants.
- Assume that troubling behavior is baby's way of telling about a need.
- An older baby *might* seek attention or power. First assume that baby is using skills he/she has to get real needs met.
- Babies do not pursue revenge or display of inadequacy.

TODDLERS

Belief	Goal	What do you usually feel/do?	How does child usually respond?	Age–level behavior	What can you do?
"I need to be noticed."	Attention	Annoyed. Nag, scold, remind.	Stops temporarily. Later, misbehaves again.	Whines.	Give attention for positive behavior. Redirect child to other activity.
"You can't make me."	Power	Angry. Punish, fight back, or give in.	Continues to misbehave, defies you.	Answers your request with "NO!"	Give choices so child can make decision.
"You don't love me!"	Revenge	Hurt. Get back at child.	Misbehaves even more, keeps trying.	Hits or calls you name.	Avoid feeling hurt or punishing. Build trust, respect.

PRESCHOOLERS

Belief	Goal	What do you usually feel/do?	How does child usually respond?	Age–level behavior	What can you do?
"I want to be noticed or waited on."	Attention	Annoyed. Nag, scold, remind.	Stops temporarily. Later, misbehaves again.	"Watch me now!" Seeks constant attention from you.	Give attention for positive behavior when child does not seek it. Make time each day to give child full attention.
"I am in control. You can't make me!"	Power	Angry. Punish, fight back, or give in.	Continues to misbehave, defies you.	Has temper tantrums, resists minding you.	Don't fight or give in. Let consequence occur.
"You don't love me!"	Revenge	Hurt. Get back at child.	Misbehaves even more, keeps trying.	Screams, yells "I hate you!" "You don't love me!"	Avoid feeling hurt or punishing. Build trust, respect.
"I am helpless. I can't."	Display of inadequacy	Hopeless, like giving up. Give up, agree that child is helpless.	Does not respond or improve.	Whines, says "I can't do it."	Encourage *any* efforts Don't pity.

Chart 2b

POSITIVE GOALS OF BEHAVIOR

BABIES

- Are beginning to form positive goals.
- Are learning to get some needs met through attention and power
- Are learning to be involved, take part, by cooing, playing, cuddling.

TODDLERS

Belief	Goal	What does child do?	How can you support child?
"I want to be like others."	Attention, involvement, to contribute	Copies parent sweeping, cooking, doing chores.	Notice, let child know you appreciate help.
"I can do it my way"	Power, independence	Wants to feed and undress self.	Let child do as much as possible for self.
"It's mine!"	Fairness, relationships with others	Learn's to respect another child's toy.	Encourage child to share toy when done playing with it.
"I want to do it myself."	Competence	Attempts to do things on own.	Accept child's efforts.

PRESCHOOLERS

Belief	Goal	What does child do?	How can you support child?
"I belong when I contribute."	Attention, involvement, to contribute	Starts to clear dishes, put own laundry in hamper.	Notice, let child know you appreciate help.
"I can decide for myself. I can do it."	Power, independence	Picks out clothes to wear.	Support, encourage child's at doing things for self.
"I want to cooperate and get along with others."	Fairness, relationships with others	Shares toys rather than fight over them.	Notice, appreciate child's efforts to cooperate.
"I want to succeed."	Competence	Accepts own mistakes. It fails, tries again.	Accept child's mistakes and recognize progress.

CHAPTER THREE

Building
Self-Esteem
in the Early Years

You want your child to form positive beliefs; to find positive ways to belong. Doing this will be easier for any child if the child has strong self-esteem. In fact, *self-esteem* is important for all of us—children and adults.

What Is Self-Esteem?

It is a belief that we belong and are:

- accepted
- strong and capable
- loved

Self-esteem helps our children be ready to deal with life. It helps them get through problems. Self-esteem helps children say, "I can" and "I will."

Start Now to Build Your Child's Self-Esteem

From birth to age 6, young children are forming beliefs about their self-worth. Parents can show their belief in and respect for their child. Now is an important time to do this. But how?

Show Respect

One way to help build children's self-esteem is through *respect.* Respect yourself. Treat your child with respect. In doing this, you show your child how to treat you—and others—with respect.

Here's what you will learn . . .

- Respect and encouragement can help build your child's self-esteem.

- Encouragement can help your child feel loved, accepted, respected, and valued.

- Praise and encouragement are not the same thing.

- You need to encourage yourself.

When parents believe in children, they help children believe in themselves.

Respect Yourself

When you respect yourself, your child has an example to follow. There are a number of ways to build your own self-respect. You will want to:

- Develop your own interests and goals.
- Learn what you are good at.
- Notice your *efforts*, not just your accomplishments.
- Be positive about yourself and others.
- Use your sense of humor.
- Know that you will make parenting mistakes—and that your child will probably be okay anyway.
- Take time for yourself.
- Remember that you are worthwhile just because you are you—not because you are a good parent.

Ines is 4. She breaks her new red crayon the first time she uses it. Ines cries. Red is her favorite color. Ines's mom breaks a water pipe she is trying to fix. Mom feels upset. She wanted to save money. Now she'll have to spend it. She's also got a big mess. Mom says to Ines, "Things are breaking for both of us. I feel upset and angry. I'll bet you do too."

To an adult, a broken pipe is more important than a broken crayon. But Mom has shown that Ines's problems are important. She didn't put herself down for not fixing the pipe. She also didn't put Ines down for breaking her crayon or for crying. Mom has shown respect for herself and for Ines. If Mom keeps doing this, Ines is likely to learn to respect herself and others too.

Help Your Child Learn Respect

Young children do not naturally show respect for someone else. Normally, they think only about themselves. You can't expect your child to be as respectful as an adult. But young children can learn to respect other people over time. They learn this when we treat them with respect.

It is never too early to begin teaching respect. How?

Be considerate. Show that you love and value your child. Consider your child's feelings:

- "You're mad that Kitty won't play. She wants to go sleep now."
- "Look at that smile! I'm glad to see you too!"

- "I know you're sad that you lost your teddy bear. Let's talk about it."

Appreciate what's special. Notice the unique things about your child:

- "What a loud, happy voice I hear coming from your crib! You like to talk, don't you?"
- "Your hand is just the right size to reach behind the dresser. Can you find the ball that rolled under there?"
- "You draw such pretty flowers! Let's send this picture to Grandma!"

Support your child's interests. Take an interest in what your child enjoys doing:

- "You like to build things. Let's make something with your blocks."
- "I know you like Curious George. We can get another book about him at the library."

Give choices. This is a way of encouraging positive power:

- "Sounds like you're hungry! Shall we warm up the corn or the squash?"
- "Would you like to wear the green shirt or the yellow shirt today?"

Help your child learn from mistakes. Mistakes can teach. Help your child learn not to fear them:

- "I didn't use enough flour in these cookies. Next time, I'll know how much flour to use."
- "Your milk got knocked off the table. Next time, you'll know not to put it so close to the edge. Here's a sponge. Let's clean it up."

Show respect for yourself. This sets a good example for your child:

- "I fixed the broken door the best I could. I'm glad it works better now."
- "I had a nice long walk—that helped me feel good today!"

It is never too early to teach respect.

Learn to Use Encouragement

Along with respect, you can encourage your child to grow in self-esteem.

What Is Encouragement?

Encouragement is a skill to help children grow in self-esteem. It is a way to show children that they belong and are:

- accepted
- strong and capable
- loved

Look at the words *encourage* and *discourage*. They both include the word courage. *Courage* is an important part of self-esteem.

The child has the courage to grow, learn, and try new things. A discouraged child has little self-esteem. The child doesn't have the courage to choose positive ways to belong or to grow, learn, and try new things.

Encouragement helps children learn to believe in themselves. It teaches them to find their own strengths and special qualities.

With encouragement, you don't ask your child to be perfect. Instead, you notice effort and improvement. You show that you accept your child. By taking the focus off comparing children with others, you help your child appreciate his or her unique individual qualities.

Corey and Nalren are cousins. They are both 11 months old. They look alike, but they act differently. At family gatherings, Corey is always moving. He checks out everything he sees. He is quick and determined. Nalren sits and smiles and babbles. If he has a toy to play with, he's happy.

The families of Corey and Nalren want to encourage both boys. They do this by appreciating each one. They see that each boy has special qualities. They love these differences and don't make negative comparisons. They say to each child, "You sure look like you're having fun."

With parent's encouragement, children learn to please *themselves*. They don't depend on pleasing other people to feel good about their efforts.

Lai, who is 5, is learning to print, She shows her dad and says, "What do you think? Did I do a good job?" Dad says, "What you think about your printing is most important. Do you like the letters you've made? I can see you're working hard. You seem to be having fun."

This response might sound unnatural. But it is encouraging. It helps Lai decide how she feels about her work. It shows her that she does not need to please someone else to feel happy with herself.

How Can I Encourage My Child?

Work to get into the encouragement habit. You can learn and practice some skills to show that you:

- Love and accept your child.
- Have faith in your child.
- Notice effort and improvement.
- Appreciate your child.

Love and Accept Your Child

Children grow at different rates. They can do different things. They also have different interests. Each child has her or his own ups and downs, strengths and weaknesses. Each child is unique.

It is important to appreciate and accept all of a child's qualities. When we do, our children see that we don't expect them to be perfect. They see that we love and value them, just for *being*.

Have Faith in Your Child

Use words and actions that show you believe in your child:

- "Go ahead—you can reach the ball by yourself."
- "You're learning to tie your shoelaces."

Notice Effort and Improvement

Learn to appreciate the large and small strides your child makes:

- "Look at that! You got the spoon to your mouth!"
- "You're remembering to wash your hands before supper."

Appreciate Your Child

Notice positive behavior. Show that you see and value your child's strengths and special qualities:

- "Sharing your toys with your cousins was nice. Did you have fun together?"

Encouragement helps children learn to believe in themselves.

• "Maybe you could sing to your baby brother. He might have an easier time falling asleep. He likes to hear you sing."

What Is the Difference Between Encouragement and Praise?

Many parents believe they are encouraging children when they praise them. They don't realize that praise can be discouraging. Praise and encouragement are not the same thing. Each one has a different purpose.

Praise Is a Reward

Praise is a type of reward. Children earn it. Praise from a parent rewards a child with being valued by the parent.

Encouragement Is a Gift

Encouragement is a gift. No one needs to earn it. It is for everyone. Encouragement can be given for effort or improvement. It can also

Praise and encouragement are not the same thing.

be given as a way of noticing what is special. It can be given at any time, even when a child is struggling or facing failure.

Four-year-old Eva paints a picture. She shows it to her mom. Mom isn't sure what the drawing is supposed to be. But she tells Eva, "Wow! This is a wonderful picture! You did a great job on it! I'm very proud of you!"

Eva may be happy with this response. She may also be learning that pleasing others is important. Nothing is wrong with wanting to please someone. But with a lot of praise, Eva may start to believe that she *must* please other people. She may decide this is the way to feel worthwhile. She may become "hooked" on praise.

Luke, who is 3 years old, draws a picture. He shows it to Ben, his stepfather. Ben looks at it carefully. Then he says to Luke, "I can tell you're happy with your picture. I see you like to use red and green."

Luke's stepfather is encouraging Luke to appreciate his own efforts. He wants Luke to learn to please himself. Ben could also ask Luke to tell him about the picture first. This would give Luke a chance to share his ideas and feelings about it.

Does this mean that you should never praise your child? No. There are times when praise can be helpful.

Leah is 2 1/2. She has had her first full day of using the toilet with no accidents in between. At bedtime her father tells her, "Good for you, Leah! You used the potty every time today!" Leah beams happily. This kind of praise is effective because it says what the child did. It is specific.

Leah feels good about her accomplishment. From the beginning, her family has noticed her efforts and her progress. The first time Leah used the toilet, they smiled and asked her, "Did you like using the potty like Mommy and Daddy?" When she wet her pants, no one made an issue of it. Instead, her mother said, "Looks like you need some dry pants. Why don't you go get them from your drawer. I'll help you clean up."

Over weeks and months, this kind of encouragement has helped Leah. She has made a successful change from diapers to the toilet—at her own speed. Tonight, her father's praise is helpful. Why? Because Leah knows her family loves and accepts her—regardless of when or how well she learns to use the toilet.

Parents who know only the language of praise can add the language of encouragement.

Praise Uses Words That Judge

"You're such a good kid!" This is not an easy thing to live up to. Hearing this, a child might think, "Am I supposed to be good all the time? What if I'm not good? Am I bad?"

"I'm so proud of you!" Hearing this, a child might hear, "You please me by doing what I want." The child might worry, "What if I don't make Daddy and Mommy proud?"

Encouragement Uses Words That Notice

Encouragement focuses on how a child has helped. It looks at how the child feels. To encourage a child, you might say:

- "Thank you for being patient at the store."

- "You seem proud that you can write your name."

The Language of Encouragement

Encouragement has its own language. Here are some examples of phrases that encourage young children:

- "You seem to like that."

- "How do you feel about it?"

- "You can do it."

- "Thanks. That helped me a lot."

- "I need your help on _____."

- "You really worked hard on that!"

- "You're getting better at _____."."

- "I really appreciate your help."

- "You're really making progress."

A Word of Caution

Sometimes parents say something encouraging, but then add something discouraging. For example, a parent might say, "It looks like you really worked hard on that." A child would feel encouraged. But what if the parent added phrases like these?

- "You worked hard on that . . . I wish you always would."

- "You can do it . . . if you quit whining and get busy."

OH JENNA...
GET OUT THE
PEANUTS!

Look for ways to support your child's interests.

Statements like these give encouragement——and then take it away. The child ends up feeling *dis*couraged. Remember that you are building your child's self-esteem. You are not trying to help your child be perfect!

How Can I Help My Child Grow and Learn?

You are your child's first teacher. You want your child to:

- Learn how to face changes and challenges.
- Develop skills.
- Enjoy learning.

How can you do this *without* praising or pushing? Don't be concerned with how your child *performs*. Instead, be interested in helping your child *learn how* to *learn*.

Guidelines for Encouraging Learning

Provide safe opportunities to learn. Give your baby lots of space to crawl and explore safely. Let your toddler scribble, paint, and

You want to encourage your children to learn. You <u>don't</u> want to push.

build. Make sure your preschooler has opportunities to play with other children.

Follow your child's interest. Your child might love elephants. Find books about them. Ask your child to tell you stories about them.

Watch for chances for learning. At the park, point out animals and flowers. At the post office, talk with your child about what people are doing.

Ask open-ended questions. *Open-ended* questions have no simple, single answer. They encourage your child to think, explain, and explore:

- "What do you think the squirrel will do with that acorn?"
- "How did you make your block tower so tall?"

Notice and encourage. "You did that all by yourself! You're happy you can button your shirt."

Help your child accept and learn from mistakes. Mistakes are part of learning. Encourage your child to keep at it: "Oops—you dropped the ball. That's okay. Let's try again."

Make learning fun. Make games out of learning to count, dress, or climb stairs.

Help your child see another point of view. Sometimes learning and exploring can be hard. Things can go wrong. There is almost always a way to see things differently:

- "I know you're scared of the thunder. Let's look at this book about storms. Maybe we'll find out why they're so noisy."
- "It's hard to pick up all these toys at once. Why don't you start with putting the trucks in the cupboard?" When your child is done with that, suggest the next step: "No more trucks? That was quick! What part can you pick up next?"

You want to *encourage* your children to learn. You *don't* want to push. Many parents want their children to be the best. They want them to be ready to reach high goals in learning. They'd like them to perform music and to dance. They want them to compete in sports. These parents push their children hard and fast.

When parents do this, they mean well. But children pay a price for such pressure. They may start to worry about how they perform. Maybe they believe they're not "good enough." They may get or fake headaches and stomachaches. Perhaps they fight or give up.

We encourage learning when we:

- Set reasonable goals with the child.

- Accept the child's efforts.

- Appreciate the child's improvements.

Chart 3, "Encouraging Young Children," shows ways to encourage learning instead of pushing.

How Can I Show Love to My Child?

Children need to know they are loved. Then they believe they are *lovable*. This builds their self-esteem. Respect and encouragement are ways to show our children that we love them. Here are some more ways to say "I love you":

Just say it. Give the message every day, to every child:

- "Good morning, Tommy. I love you."

- "Guess who loves you as big as a mountain? Guess who loves you as high as the moon?"

- "Let's name all the people who love you: Grandfather, Rashida, Aunt Opal . . ."

For babies and young children, touch is more powerful than any words.

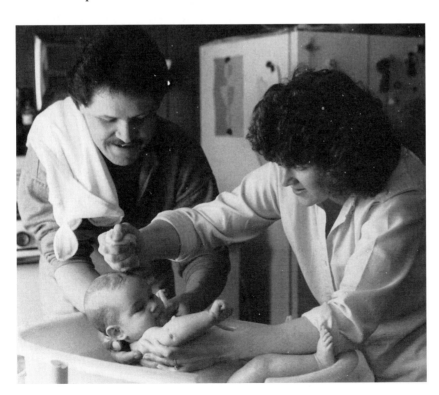

Show appreciation:

- "Good night, Elizabeth. I liked my day with you. I'll be happy to see you when you wake up."
- "Miguel, you're such a snuggly snuggler! It's fun to snuggle with you."
- "Oh my, you're getting big! I love to watch you grow and learn."

Spend time with your child. This means a time when you set everything else aside. Turn off the TV. Put down your work. Give your child your complete attention. You might do something you both enjoy.

In our pressured, adult world, finding time to do this can be hard. It's worth the effort! Your child will get the message, "I'm important." And you and your child will enjoy being together.

Guide behavior with respect. It's hard to say too much about the importance of respect! When our children make mistakes or misbehave, we need to stay respectful. What we say and do at these times affects their self-esteem too. If we yell or make fun of them, our efforts to show love can easily be undone.

Show love through touch. For babies and young children, touch is more powerful than any words. In caring for babies, we use a lot of body contact. We bathe, dress, change, and feed them. The way we hold and caress our babies can very clearly tell them that they are loved.

Toddlers and preschoolers often push away from our hugs and kisses. But they still need a parent's loving touch. Every day, we have many chances to give it. We help our children dress themselves. We might teach them how to wash. We tuck them in at night. At all of these times, gentle, caring touch says, "I love you."

Sometimes your child will say, "No, I don't want a hug." That's okay. Respect your child's feelings. At other times, your child will climb onto your lap and just want to be held. Physical games—like chase and wrestling—are another chance for loving touch. Young children love to bounce, roll, fall, and bump together. You show love through both playful and gentle touch.

A Word About Neglect and Abuse

The right words and touches show love to children. If we don't give loving words and touches, our children will feel *neglected*. They can't learn love and respect from us if we don't show it.

Listen to your child's feelings about child care. Answer questions. Explain that your child will be safe.

The wrong words and touches can hurt self-esteem. They tell children we think they are bad. They tell children we have power to hurt them. These words and touches are abusive.

Parents don't want to neglect or abuse their children. But all parents feel overworked or angry at times.

I'm Really Angry—What Should I Do?

1. **Get away from your child.** Leave the room. Go for a walk. Call a friend. If you can't leave your child alone, call a friend and ask for help.

2. **Seek help for yourself.** If you are so angry that you are afraid you will hurt your child, there are people who can help you. You can check with a neighborhood center, counselor, or social worker. You can call a doctor's office. You can call a religious organization. You can ask a teacher for the name of someone to call. You can look in the phone book under "Crisis Numbers."

Encouragement and Child Care

Your child is not always with you. Choose child care that fits your parenting style. You want to know that anyone who cares for your child will show love and respect.

Ideas for Child Care and Activities

Here are some types of child care and away-from-home activities to think about:

- Have a friend or relative care for your child.

- Hire someone to come into your home.

- Place your child in a family day-care home, child-care center, or preschool.

- Join an Early Childhood Family Enrichment (ECFE) program. Many states in the U.S. have these programs. Parents have a chance to meet and talk to other parents. Children spend time learning with other children and loving adults. Ask your local school or community center about your nearest ECFE.

- Look for "Mother's Day Out" programs in your community.

- Look for a Head Start program. Most communities have Head Start.

Encouragement
STEP

All people—parents and children—have strengths. Sometimes seeing a young child's strengths is hard. Maybe your child plays well with others, is friendly, or has a nice smile. Think about these strengths as "seeds." Seeds need water and sunlight to grow. Think of encouragement as water and sunlight.

This week, find one "seed" of strength in your child. Use encouragement to "water" that seed as often as you can.

Choosing Child Care

When choosing child care or activities, keep these questions in mind:

- **Is the home or center safe?** Inside, look for child safety gates, covered sockets, locked cupboards, and age-level toys. Outside, look for a fenced yard and play equipment that will be safe for your child's age.

- **Can you trust the caregiver?** The caregiver you choose should enjoy being with young children. Also find out if he or she has training in child development, nutrition, safety, and health.

- **Are there interesting toys and materials?** Are there activities to help children learn to get along? Do the children seem happy and involved? A good program won't use a lot of television to keep children busy.

- **Do you agree on discipline?** daily routines? important values? Before you choose, visit the home or center at least once—more if possible. Talk to other parents too. Get to know the caregivers or teachers. The caregivers need to be *consistent* about encouragement, respect, and discipline. They should encourage learning without pushing.

- **How much can parents be involved?** When your child is in a program, you should be able to visit at any time—without an appointment.

- **What are your community's licensing requirements?** Licensing helps you know your child will be safe. But it doesn't guarantee a quality program. You'll need to make this judgment. Keep in mind your goals. Trust your feelings.

- **How many children are there for each adult?** Research shows that both smaller groups and fewer children for each caregiver are better for children. The National Association for the Education of Young Children (NAEYC) recommends *one adult for every three infants, four to five toddlers, or eight to nine preschoolers.*

Before your toddler or preschooler enters any child-care situation, talk about it together. Listen to your child's feelings. Answer questions. Explain that your child will be safe. Take your child for a visit to meet the caregivers, teachers, and other children. Do this before you sign your child up.

Have the Courage to Be Imperfect

Thinking about all this, you may wonder, "How can I possibly do it all? What if I make a mistake?"

It may help if you remind yourself that you can't always show respect or be encouraging. No one can! Like all parents, you will make mistakes as you raise your child. But keep thinking about respect. Reminding yourself to encourage your child as much as you can will help too.

Also encourage *yourself.* It is important to do this. Recognize what you are doing well. Focus on what helps you feel good about yourself.

Earlier, we talked about the word *courage.* Rudolf Dreikurs had an idea he called *the courage to be imperfect.* With the courage to be imperfect, you:

- Accept yourself as you are.

- See mistakes as part of learning.

- Enjoy yourself, your child, and other people. This feels much better than finding fault.

- Make small changes—not try to be a whole new you.

- Get to know your own strengths and good qualities.

- Value yourself.

- See parenting as a challenge to be met—not a problem to overcome.

With strong self-esteem, you help your child develop self-esteem. With the courage to face life's challenges, you help your child develop courage too.

THIS WEEK

This week, find ways to encourage your child. Find as many ways as you can. Each time, notice:

- what happened
- how you encouraged your child
- how your child responded

Encourage yourself too:

- Focus on your own strengths, efforts, and improvements.
- Keep using positive self-talk.

POINTS *TO* REMEMBER

1. Respect and encouragement help children develop self-esteem.

2. You encourage when you:
    *   Love and accept your child.
    *   Have faith in your child.
    *   Notice effort and improvement.
    *   Appreciate your child.

3. Encouragement is a gift. Everyone deserves it. It can be given for effort, when a child is not doing well, and for just *being*.

4. Help your children learn *how* to learn. Don't teach them they need to be perfect.

5. Don't push children. Encourage them by setting reasonable goals, accepting their efforts, and appreciating their improvements.

6. Show your love for your child:
    *   Say "I love you."
    *   Show appreciation.
    *   Spend time with your child.
    *   Guide behavior with respect.
    *   Show love through touch.

7. You want to know that anyone who cares for your child will show love and respect.

8. Encourage yourself, and have the courage to be imperfect.

JUST FOR YOU

Your Adult Relationships

As you work to encourage your child, don't lose sight of your close adult relationships. Set aside time to be with your spouse, friend, or sister or brother. You might do one of these things:

- Talk together alone.
- Take walks.
- Ride bikes or play a sport together (but leave time to talk).
- Have a picnic.
- Have lunch or dinner together.
- Go out for coffee.
- Get away for a weekend.

During your time together, set aside thoughts of the children. Instead, focus on your relationship. Listen to each other. Share feelings. Encourage each other. Have fun together.

What will you do this week to have fun with another adult?

Chart 3

CHAPTER THREE 59

ENCOURAGING YOUNG CHILDREN

You *do* want to encourage.
You *don't* want to push.

Age	Do	Don't
BABIES	Allow infant to explore at own pace.	Overstimulate. Dont force infant to be near animals when he/she is afraid.
	Give infant age-level toys.	Give toys that are too hard, dangerous (examples: so small that infant could swallow, unsafe to put in mouth, have sharp edges).
	Allow infant to grow, develop at own rate.	Coax infant to crawl or walk before physically ready or able.
	Help infant give up breast or bottle when she/he shows interest in cup.	Force infant to give up breast or bottle before ready.
TODDLERS	Help toddler start toilet training when he/she seems interested, physically able.	Force toddler to use potty or start toilet training when she/he is not interested or physically able.
	Help toddler give up pacifier or blanket when interested, ready.	Take away pacifier or blanket when toddler still depends on it.
	Guide toddler to behave appropriately for age (example: learn to eat with knife and fork).	Demand that toddler act in more mature way than he/she is able.
PRESCHOOLERS	Encourage child to learn age-level skills.	Teach skills, ideas that are beyond child's age level.
	Set stage for creative play.	Set strict "rules" for play (example: expecting child not to be messy with fingerpaints).
	Encourage child to try new things. Stress that mistakes are okay.	Stress doing things "right." Expect perfection.

CHAPTER FOUR

Listening *and* Talking

to Young Children

We want to show our children respect. *Respectful communication* is the key to most relationships. Think about what this means in a friendship.

You and your friend Jerry are watching TV. Jerry knocks his soft drink over onto the carpet. Embarrassed, he says, "Oh, no! Look what I did to your rug!" You get some towels to clean the mess. You say, "Don't worry, Jerry—this carpet has seen a lot worse!"

When our friends have problems or make mistakes, we think about their feelings. We do this because we respect and value our friends. Treating our children the same way will help us build a closer relationship.

When you're upset, you might talk to a friend about it. You'd like your friend to listen. You want your friend to understand and accept what you are feeling. Your child wants this from you too.

Talking is one way children communicate. But young children don't have a lot of words. Look at what your child's face and body are telling you. Be aware of your own "body language" too. Your actions show *your* feelings. They show whether you understand and respect your child.

How Can I Be a Good Listener?

Communication has two main parts: listening and talking. You can make it easier for your child to communicate with you. How? By showing that you care enough to listen and to speak respectfully to your child.

Here's what you will learn . . .

- Listening and talking respectfully to your child are important.

- Listening to hear how your child is feeling is a skill you can learn.

- You can show your child that expressing feelings is okay.

- You can talk about problems without blaming.

I'M SORRY-- UNTIL YOU TWO CAN LEARN TO DRINK COFFEE WITHOUT SPILLING YOU'LL HAVE TO USE THE TOMMY TIPPY CUPS!

Imagine if we talked to our friends as we sometimes do to our children.

Treat your child as you'd treat your best friend.

Parents need to do a lot of listening. If you listen well, your child will feel understood. You help your child learn ways to deal with feelings and problems. Also, you show your child how to become a good listener.

Listening starts when you respond to your infant's first cry. A baby's cries communicate many things: hunger, tiredness, pain, boredom, and fear. You also need to "listen" with your eyes—for babies soon begin to use body language. Your baby's smile may say, "I'm happy." Pulling away may say, "I'm angry!"

As babies grow, they learn which sounds and actions get parents' attention. A toddler knows how to pull an adult to the kitchen and point out a favorite food. Sometime after their first year, most children begin to use words. Later, the words come together into full sentences.

Young children ask us to listen for many reasons. Most of what they tell us is clear and simple: "I want a cookie." Our responses are also simple and clear: "Yes, you may" or "No, you may not." This kind of listening is easy.

Sometimes what children want us to understand may not be so clear. They may have feelings they don't know how to express.

During breakfast, your 2 year old has been happy. Suddenly he frowns and shouts "No!" You ask him, "Are you done eating?" He shouts "No!" again and starts to cry. You can tell he's unhappy but don't know why. You ask, "Can you tell me what's wrong?" He pulls on his ear and cries, "Ear! Bad!" You say, "Your ear hurts?" He holds his ear and cries, "Ear hurt!" Gently, you pick up your toddler. "Let's find the thermometer," you say. "If your ear is sick, we'll have to make it better."

The way you listen and talk about feelings can show your child how to communicate with respect. You need to hear, understand, and accept your child's feelings. Then slowly, over the years to come, your child will begin to understand other people's feelings too.

Listen for Feelings

Listening for feelings is a special skill. It is called *reflective listening*.

Using reflective listening shows that you value your child's feelings. It's a way to tell your child that you understand the meaning behind your child's words and body language. Reflective listening shows that you *want to understand*.

How to Use Reflective Listening

1. **Listen.** Let your body show that you are listening. Stop your other tasks. Look directly at your child. Sit or kneel next to your child so you will be at your child's level. You might have to pick up your child so you are face-to-face.

2. **Hear the feeling.** Listen to your child's words. Ask yourself, "What is my child feeling?" Think of a word that describes the feeling.

3. **Say what you've heard.** Think of yourself as a kind of mirror that *reflects* your child's feelings. You also reflect what you think is the *reason behind* the feeling.

To reflect the feeling, start by using the words "You feel" and "because":

- "*You feel* excited *because* Marta's coming for supper."

- "*You feel* tired *because* you worked so hard."

After a while, reflective listening will feel more natural. Then you may want to use your own words:

- "You're sorry that Mikey got hurt."

- "You like playing with Keesha, don't you?"

After a morning of fun in the park, your 3 year old starts to whimper. Dragging her feet, she says, "I don't wanna go home!" You use reflective listening. You say, "You're disappointed that our playtime is over. You were having so much fun."

The way you listen and talk about feelings teaches your child about respect.

What if you aren't sure about what your child is feeling? Guessing is okay.

Your son comes home from kindergarten. He is scowling. He says, "School is dumb!" You say, "Sounds like you're angry about something that happened at school today." He says, "No, I'm not angry. But the teacher doesn't like me." Then he begins to tell you what happened with the teacher.

What if you had said, "You shouldn't talk that way! School isn't dumb!" Your son might believe his feelings aren't okay. He might not feel safe to tell you what happened.

Help Children Find the Words

Children need to know many words for feelings. Then they can talk about how they feel. When you use reflective listening, you teach children to name their feelings.

Five feeling words parents use too much are *good, bad, happy, sad,* and *mad.* These words don't always tell the whole story.

Look at this list of words. Think of as many other feeling words as you can.

Words for "Happy" Feelings

appreciate	enjoy	great	nice
better	excited	happy	pleased
cheerful	glad	like	proud
delighted	good	love	wonderful

Words for "Upset" Feelings

angry	disappointed	hurt	sad
annoyed	frightened	irritated	scared
confused	guilty	left out	sorry

When Should I Use Reflective Listening?

Reflective listening may be new to both you and your child. Here are some hints to help you.

Listen for strong feelings. Sometimes your child will use strong language or actions. Your child *may* use body language—crying, hitting, stiffening, laughing, hugging. Or your child *may* use strong words—"I hate you!" "I'm going to run away!" "You're the best mom in the world!"

Children need to know many words for feelings. Then they can talk about how they feel.

When you see or hear these strong feelings, use reflective listening. "You feel very mad." "You're really excited that Vic is coming over." This can help your child understand the feelings. It helps your child know that the feelings are okay.

Listen for hidden feelings. Sometimes you know your child's feelings are below the surface. Then using reflective listening is also helpful.

Your 4 year old watches two hours of TV. After that, she goes from room to room, doing nothing. Then she demands more TV. You say: "It looks like you may be feeling bored. Let's think about some things you could do."

This may help your child recognize her feeling. She may be better able to think of other choices for herself.

Reflective listening helps when you have to say no. Sometimes you have to say no to your child. When you do, your child may cry or yell. Use reflective listening in that situation. Then your child will know you have heard the feelings:

- "I can see that you're angry because I said no TV right now."

- "I know you're mad, but the answer is still no. I'm going to put a load of laundry in the washer now."

- "I can hear that you're very angry with me. That's okay—you can say 'I'm angry at you, Mommy.' But I won't answer you when you call me names."

Reflective listening helps your child know that showing feelings is okay.

Once you explain your limits, ignore any more name-calling. If this is hard to do, you may have to remove the child from the room. You could explain, "I see you've decided not to be around people."

Reflective listening isn't always necessary. Often, children's messages are clear and simple. A child may say, "I want some milk." The words hold no hidden meaning.

Sometimes you can't listen. Young children think they are the center of the world. This is natural. They may want you to listen all the time. That isn't possible—or desirable! If you don't have time to listen, say so. Tell the child you can talk later: "I can see you're excited and want to tell me all about the zoo. But I have to make a phone call first. Can you tell me more about it after I finish?"

How Can I Talk So My Child Will Listen?

You have seen how listening and talking go together: You listen for feelings. Then you say what you hear. Besides reflecting your child's feelings, you also need to talk about your own. Let's look at how to tell your child about *your* feelings.

Speak With Respect and Encouragement

When you have a problem with your child, you need to talk about it. When you do, share your feelings respectfully—without being judgmental.

Sid and Tessa are 4 years old. Their daddies are busy putting up curtain rods. Tessa and Sid run all around the apartment. They grow noisy. Next, they ask their dads for a snack. Then they want a shoe tied. Then they want help finding a lost toy.

Sid's daddy says, "Quit being such a pest, Sid. How can I ever get this work done?" Tessa's daddy tells his daughter, "When there's so much noise, it takes longer to get done here. When I'm finished, then I can get you a snack."

I-messages don't label or blame. They simply tell how you feel.

Sid's father has lashed out at his son. It's easy to see why—working can be hard when children make noise and get in the way. But being called a "pest" is discouraging for Sid.

Tessa's father is encouraging. He responds to her needs but also sets his limits. He shows her that right now he has to work. He lets Tessa know that he expects her to cooperate.

Will Tessa decide to cooperate? If she does, her father might later tell her, "It helped me when you played quietly today while I finished my work." If she doesn't, he can use respectful words to let her know her behavior is not appropriate.

What kind of respectful words can we use? One way to talk about problems is with an I-message.

Use an I-Message

When talking to children, we can use "you-messages" or "I-messages."

You-messages put down, blame, or nag. Often they use the word *you*: "You should know better."

Children who hear too many you-messages can begin to feel worthless. They may fight back or stop listening. You-messages are discouraging. They can lower self-esteem. Also, they don't teach children about cooperation.

I-messages show respect. A better way to talk about a problem is with an I-message. I-messages tell how *you*, the parent, feel when a child ignores your rights. Rather than focusing on the child, I-messages focus on you. I-messages don't label or blame. When you use an I-message, you simply tell how you feel.

I-Messages Have Three Parts

To use an I-message, you do three things:

1. Tell what is happening.

2. Tell how you feel.

3. Explain why you feel that way.

Here is an I-message:

- "When I see hitting, I feel worried because somebody could get hurt."

It uses these words:

1. When   "*When* I see hitting,

2. I feel   I *feel* worried

3. Because   *because* somebody could get hurt."

- "*When* toys are left on the rug, I *feel* discouraged *because* I have to pick them up before I can vacuum."

- "*When* I hear so much crying, I *feel* confused *because* I can't understand what you're trying to say to me."

An I-message shows respect for you. It lets you be honest about how you feel and what you want. I-messages show respect for your child. They show that you expect cooperation.

Use I-messages when you are speaking with an older toddler or a preschooler. With a younger child, you may want to speak in a simpler way:

- "I don't like having my nose pulled. It hurts."

- "I get a headache listening to so much noise."

Remember these things about I-messages:

- They focus on *you*, not your child.

- They do not place blame on anyone.

Let's look at more examples of I-messages.

Two-year-old Carmen runs into the street. Rushing after her, Mom carries Carmen back to the sidewalk. She tells her daughter, "I get scared when you run into the street. A car could hit you, and you could get very badly hurt."

Carmen is too young really to understand how her mom feels. But she can sense the feelings behind her mom's tone of voice.

Pedro and Zach are 4. Pedro won't share his toys with Zach. Pedro's mother says, "Pedro, when you decide not to let Zach play with your toys, I feel disappointed, because there's fighting. And it looks like Zach feels hurt that you won't share."

Mother's I-message may not solve the problem. But Pedro gets to hear how his actions affect two people. This can help him focus on solving the problem.

Avoid Angry I-Messages

Keeping angry feelings out of your I-messages is important. It's hard for children *not* to feel blamed when you express anger.

Often anger is only part of the feeling. For example, you may start out feeling disappointed. But you don't say anything. Instead, you focus on how disappointed you feel. Slowly, you begin to feel angry. No matter what you say, your anger will show.

You can avoid angry I-messages. How? By stating the feelings linked to your anger.

You are in the store with your 3 year old. She wanders off. You're afraid something has happened to her. By the time you find her, you feel very angry. But you decide not to act on your anger. Instead, you express your fear. Giving your child a hug, you say, "Thank goodness you're safe! I was really scared something had happened to you! Please stay close to Daddy."

Can you assume that your child has learned her lesson about safety? No. Children need safety guidelines stated again and again, over many years. Remember, young children won't necessarily understand the problem from your point of view. Still, using I-messages helps your child feel respected. It shows that you value your child enough to deal with a problem without yelling, blaming, or threatening.

Send Friendly I-Messages Too!

Children love to hear friendly I-messages! They are a wonderful way to encourage:

- "It sure feels good to come home to your happy smile today."

- "I noticed when you let Samol hold your doll. It's nice to see you're learning to share."

- "I'm happy when you clean up your spilled juice. It shows you can do it yourself."

Keep Your Expectations Realistic

Reflective listening and I-messages will help you communicate with your child. They will help you to guide—not control. Even when

Respectful communication takes time.

Notice when your child tries to do something positive. Focus on effort. Give encouragement. For example:

- *"You're spending a lot of time building that tower."*

- *"You seem to like helping me fix supper."*

- *"You put the puzzle together! You worked so hard. It feels good to figure it out, doesn't it?"*

Notice especially when your child tries to cooperate.

children feel respected, they may not stop unpleasant behavior. Don't give up! Your child is learning to communicate. This takes time.

When Should I Start Using Reflective Listening and I-Messages?

You can begin using reflective feelings and I-messages with infants. Very young children will miss the meaning of your words. But they *won't* miss the kindness and respect in your voice and face:

- "I see you like your bath."

- "Oh—you reached for the rattle!"

- "When you pull the kitty's tail, it hurts her."

- "If you open your mouth, the food will go in easier. And you won't feel so mad and hungry."

Starting early also gives you practice. Then, when your child begins to talk, you will already be used to listening and speaking in these ways. Reflective listening and I-messages will help you begin a respectful relationship with your child—from the start.

THIS WEEK

Start to notice what you *first* want to say when your child talks to you or misbehaves. Stop yourself from talking before thinking.

Instead, think of respectful ways to talk with your child. Do these as often as you can:

- Use reflective listening.

- Use I-messages.

- Be sure to reflect and say positive feelings too.

POINTS TO REMEMBER

1. Young children use body language long before they can speak.

2. Sometimes children don't have the words to express their feelings.

3. When you use reflective listening, you reflect your child's feeling and the reason for the feeling:

   - "You *feel* sorry *because* Mikey got hurt."

   - "You *feel* excited *because* Marta's coming for supper."

4. Children need to hear and learn words for their feelings.

5. You-messages put down or blame. I-messages tell how you feel without blaming.

6. To use an I-message, tell what is happening, how you feel, and why you feel that way. Use these words:

   - When   "*When* I see hitting,

   - I feel   I *feel* worried

   - because   *because* somebody could get hurt."

7. Avoid using angry I-messages.

8. Reflective listening and I-messages are ways to communicate respect.

9. It will take time for your child to learn to talk and act respectfully. Don't give up.

JUST FOR YOU

"Straight Talk" for Adults

Respectful communication between you and your child is important. It's also important between you and other adults.

Suppose it's your night to wash the dishes. Your spouse or a friend puts dirty plates and pans in the sink without rinsing them. You could say: "When the dishes aren't rinsed, I get discouraged, because it's extra hard to get them clean."

What if you get no response? Make a clear statement about what you want: "I'd prefer the dishes be rinsed so I can wash them up quickly."

I-messages and clear statements about what you want let you do three things:

- You say what it is that you want—"I want a hug." "I would like some time to talk."

- You tell what *you* will do—"I'll wash what I find in the hamper." "I'll cook supper if you'll make the salad."

- You are friendly and respectful—even when you are firm.

Think of a problem you have had with your spouse or a friend. You may have been silent when you needed to speak. Or maybe you spoke, but in a blaming way. How could you have said what you meant in a better way?

This week, practice saying what you mean. Don't overdo it—take it one step at a time.

Chart 4 CHAPTER FOUR 73

REFLECTIVE LISTENING AND I-MESSAGES

	Reflective Listening	**I-Messages**
Babies Babies won't understand all your words. They will sense your feelings.	"You can't reach the ball—you feel angry." "You're scared the doggy will bite." "You're very happy to have your bear."	"When you feel sick, I feel sad." "When I see you smiling, I feel happy too!" "I wish I knew why you were crying."
Toddlers Toddlers have more words. Watch their actions for feelings too.	"You sound angry with me because I said no cookies." "You're really excited to get to play." "You face says you're sad––do you think this is unfair?"	"When I don't know why you're crying, I don't know how to help." "When you say you don't love me, I feel sad, but I still love you." "When you throw toys, I worry that something might get broken."
Preschoolers Preschoolers have better reasoning abilities. Keep watching their actions for feelings. Use *exact* feeling words. Guess if you need to.	"You look disappointed about not winning the game. Want to talk about it?" "Is it possible that you're feeling left out?" "It's nice to feel like the teacher appreciated your help at circle time."	"I feel good when you put your toys away. It shows that you want to help." "Running on the wet sidewalk scares me. It's slippery. You might fall and get hurt." "When you play nicely with your friends, I feel happy. You're showing me you can get along with others."

CHAPTER FIVE

Helping
Young Children
Learn to Cooperate

We want our children to become responsible adults. To live, work, and play with others, children must learn to cooperate. One of our jobs as parents is to teach cooperation. We do this by cooperating ourselves. When we do this, we show our children what cooperating means.

What Is Cooperation?

Parents sometimes use the word *cooperate* when they mean *obey*:

Jenna, who is 3, is fooling around at supper. When she sings, her father says, "Stop singing at the table, Jenna." She feeds the cat under the table. She grabs her sister's toast. Her father says, "Leave your sister and the cat alone." Jenna keeps fooling around. "Jenna, eat your dinner!" exclaims her father. Jenna ignores him. Dad is fed up. He yells at Jenna, "I want you to cooperate, young lady! Sit still and eat— or else! And not another word out of you!"

Dad says he wants cooperation. But what he really wants is for Jenna to obey. Yelling and threats might make her mind—for a while. But Dad could show Jenna something more useful: to cooperate with him and the other people in her home.

Cooperation is working together. It doesn't mean that children do what adults order them to do. There are many ways to help our children learn to cooperate.

Here's what you will learn . . .

- Cooperation means working together.

- Your child is learning about cooperation. Learning takes time.

- Cooperation needs patience and encouragement.

- You and your child can solve problems by talking together.

How Much Cooperation Can I Expect?

Cooperation needs to be encouraged. What kind of cooperation can you expect from a baby? a toddler? a preschooler? What can you do to help your child learn cooperation?

Babies

Babies are explorers. They learn by using all their senses—sight, hearing, smell, touch, and taste. Babies explore without rules or common sense. In part, they explore to find limits, or *boundaries*.

Babies see themselves as the center of the universe. They don't know about the needs and rights of others. Because of this, you can't expect your baby to cooperate naturally. But babyhood is the perfect time to begin teaching cooperation. Every moment you spend with your baby is a chance to show respect and cooperation.

Pablo is 8 months old. Mom is giving him a bath. She says, "You like it when I wash your arm with the soft cloth. Now you wash my arm. I like it too!" She guides Pablo's hand to wash her arm.

Parents sometimes use the word "cooperate" when they mean "obey."

Babies can be very determined.

Nara is 5 months old. Her dad feeds her. Then he puts her in the infant seat. He says, "I fed you-now you're fine. But I'm hungry! You can help me. Keep me company and play while I eat."

Do Pablo and Nara understand their parents' words? Will the pleasant words "make" them cooperate? No. Pablo may pull on his mother's earrings. Nara may fuss and make Dad's meal unpleasant. Is this "naughty"? No. Babies are immature. However, their actions show what they want.

Babies need adults to set limits that will keep them safe. When they set limits for a child, parents teach cooperation.

If Pablo pulls at his mother's earrings, she can take them off. She can say to Pablo, "I know you don't want to hurt me-and I don't want you to! Are you ready to wash my arm now?" If he's not ready, Mother can respect that. She can simply keep on with his bath. She models cooperation as she keeps necessary limits in place.

Toddlers

Toddlers still like to explore. But they are beginning to see the results of their actions:

- "When I run, you chase me."

- "When I scream, you cringe."

- "When I cry, you hug."

Toddlers can move faster and farther than babies. But they don't have self-control or see dangers. Toddlers need clear safety limits. They also need to start learning social limits. Toddlers can *begin* to understand parents' messages about which behaviors are—and are not—okay.

Toddlers have a simple sense of what cooperation means. They often act in ways that seem totally *un*cooperative. Your toddler may:

- refuse to do what you ask

- do the opposite of what you ask

- say no—loudly and often

Toddlers are learning that they can control themselves. They show this in many ways; for example, closing their mouth when parents want them to eat or running away when parents want them to get

Toddlers are becoming more independent. They are also learning there are limits.

dressed. Are the toddlers being "bad"? No. They are learning what they can and can't do as they grow more independent.

How can you encourage your toddler to cooperate? By guiding your child to positive activities that build independence and self-esteem.

Malik is 2 1/2. His grandpa finds him playing roughly with the dog. Grandpa says, "I see you're petting the dog. She likes to be petted, doesn't she? Would you like to help me brush her? That's right—gentle, not hard. Like this."

Kim is 2. She is being loud and wild. Her mother picks her up and holds her. She tells Kim, "Running and shouting are fine outside, but not in the apartment. I need to wash dishes now. You can help me. Then we'll go to the park."

Preschoolers

Emotion rules toddlers. But reason begins to play a part in the behavior of preschoolers. Preschoolers are better able to use self-control. They have some ability to change their behavior to avoid unwanted consequences.

Preschoolers are beginning to cooperate. Encouraging this is important.

How do you get the cooperation you expect from your preschooler? Give clear, simple rules. Explain the *consequences* of breaking the rules. Your preschooler won't always understand your expectations. But this understanding is growing.

It's not reasonable to expect completely cooperative preschoolers. We can expect the *beginnings* of cooperative behavior. Preschoolers naturally believe their needs and wishes come first. But the seeds of cooperative behavior—seeds that were planted in babyhood—are beginning to sprout.

How Can I Begin to Teach Cooperation?

Problems between parents and children can't be avoided. When you have a problem with your child, you need to decide how to deal with it. First, ask yourself, "Who does this problem belong to? me? or my child?" In other words, who "owns" the problem?

Decide Who Owns the Problem

To decide who owns a problem, ask yourself four questions:

1. Are my rights being disrespected?

2. Could anybody get hurt?

3. Are someone's belongings threatened?

4. Is my child too young to be responsible for this problem?

- If the answer to *any* of these questions is "yes," then you own the problem.

- If the answer to *every* question is "no," then your child owns the problem.

With babies and young toddlers, parents own most of the problems. As children grow older, they begin to own some of the problems.

Your 9 month old has a wet diaper. This is your problem. It involves your child's safety (health).

Your 5 year old wets his pants. He has no physical problem with bladder control. He needs to change and clean himself to learn to be responsible for himself.

Your 1 year old is crying because she's hungry. This is your problem.

Your 4 year old won't eat her lunch. An hour later, she complains that she's hungry. This is her problem.

Examples of Parent-Owned Problems

Shantelle is 4. In the morning, she refuses to dress herself. She dawdles over her cereal. Shantelle's mother has trouble getting her to the sitter. Her mother is often late for work.

Dad goes to get the baby up from his nap. He finds 3-year-old Amy poking the baby and pulling his hair.

Two-year-old Ben colors on the wall in the kitchen.

Examples of Child-Owned Problems

Jarek is 2. He loves Whiskers, the cat. But whenever Jarek comes near, Whiskers runs away. Jarek bursts into tears!

Five-year-old Gia is bored. She wanders into the living room. Her stepfather is studying. Sadly she says, "There's nothing to do. Will you play with me?"

Erin and her friend Isaac are playing. Mom hears a wail. She rushes to the living room. Erin is surrounded by nearly all her toys. She is sobbing. Isaac sits a little apart. He is playing with Erin's favorite stuffed rabbit. "Rabbie," cries Erin to her mother. "I want my Rabbie!"

What About Babies?

The younger our children are, the more they depend on us for their care. Meeting their needs is our problem—they can do little for themselves.

Still, letting babies do what they can do is important. This builds their growing sense of belief in themselves.

Susie is 6 months old. She wants the rattle. But it is a few inches out of reach. She struggles to reach it. Susie's mother doesn't get the rattle for Susie. Instead, she encourages Susie's efforts to get the rattle herself.

Hungry, 3-month-old Josh cries. His dad feeds him. Later, Josh fusses in his crib at naptime. His dad doesn't go to Josh right away. He gives Josh a few minutes to comfort himself.

With babies and young toddlers, parents own most of the problems.

How Can I Help My Child Cooperate to Solve Problems?

Deciding who owns problems helps you know what to expect. It also helps you think about what to do next. If you own the problem, you need to take action. If your child owns the problem, you might want to let your child handle it. Or you might want to help your child solve the problem.

You've already learned many things to do when there's a problem. You might:

- Ignore the problem.
- Use reflective listening.
- Use an I-message.
- Help your child see the choices and the possible consequences.

Your goal is to handle the problem in a way that respects both you and your child. Children learn more about cooperation when they feel that you value their feelings and wishes. What you do will depend on:

- the child's age
- the type of problem
- how often the problem happens

Keep It Simple

Often, you can give a simple choice:

- "If you want to play at Juana's, you need to pick up your toys first."
- "Can you two solve this problem fairly, or do you need to stop playing now?"

We want our children to begin learning to count on themselves to solve some of their problems. Find ways to encourage children. Focus on helping them learn new skills and behavior.

Carl is 2 1/2. He doesn't want his parents to go out. They notice his feelings. They offer to read to him for a few minutes before they leave. Carl isn't satisfied. He screams and hits his parents. They say, "You're really angry that we're going out. We'd like to look at a book with you first. But we can't read a story unless you stop screaming, Carl. If you don't stop, we won't have time to read to you."

Children learn more about cooperation when they feel that you value their wishes.

Three-year-old Nina and her mom are at the zoo. A lion roars loudly. Nina hides behind her mother. Her mother says, "It's very scary when a lion roars like that. What would help you feel less scared?" Nina suggests they hold hands tightly. They try it. After a while, Nina relaxes a little. Her mother says, "Your idea worked. You look happier now."

Sometimes you will teach through consequences.

You pick up 16-month-old Nicholas. He knocks your glasses off. You put them back on carefully. You say, "When my glasses are knocked off, I'm afraid they'll break."

A few minutes later, Nicholas knocks the glasses off again. You gently place Nicholas on the floor. "I can't let you grab my glasses," you say, "so I'm putting you down."

Later, Nicholas wants to be picked up again. You give him another chance. You say, "Do you want to sit on my lap again? Okay. But if you grab my glasses, I will put you down."

Here, you used an I-message, stated consequences, and followed through. Nicholas is young. He hasn't had much practice at controlling his behavior. So he will probably grab the glasses again. Whenever Nicholas grabs, you put him down. He begins to learn why.

Set Needed Limits

Some preschoolers insist. They want attention "on demand." Parents feel like these demands never stop. In this situation, teaching limits is important. Stay respectful as you explain the limits: "When someone is here talking with me, I won't play with you. You may ask a short question if you need me. But I won't be spending time with you while my friend is here."

Children need to know what will happen if they don't respect the limits: "If you interrupt when I'm talking to my friend, I'll take you to your room." The child needs to know that you mean what you say.

Jealousy between sisters and brothers often needs limits too. With babies, toddlers, and preschoolers, jealousy can become dangerous. One child may harm another child. You need to protect your young child from being hurt. Make it clear that you won't allow an older child to hurt a younger child: "We don't hit people. It's dangerous. If you hit, you won't be able to be in the room with your little brother."

Be sure to encourage your older child as often as you can. Also, spend some time alone with your older child each day. Make this a special time when your attention is only on the child.

Children need to know what will happen if they don't respect the limits.

Another way to solve a problem is to *talk the problem through* with your child. You take the time to listen, talk, and agree about a way to solve the problem. This is called *exploring alternatives*.

"Talking It Through": Five Steps for Exploring Alternatives

1. **Understand the problem.** Make sure the problem is clear to both you and your child. Ask questions that help you understand. Use reflective listening. Explain the problem clearly and respectfully. State your own feelings with I-messages.

2. **Brainstorm ideas to find alternatives.** Ask your child for ways to solve the problem. Suggest your own ideas too: "What might happen if you _____?" List all the ideas.

   These ideas are the *alternatives*. Keep an open mind for this step. Don't be quick to judge the ideas.

3. **Consider the solutions.** Now is the time to judge the ideas. What does your child think of each one? What do you think?

4. **Choose a solution.** Decide on an idea you can both accept.

5. **Use the solution.** Agree to test the solution you have decided on. Decide together how long to use the idea. Plan enough time to give the idea a fair test. Set a time to talk about the idea again.

Children who can write their names may like the idea of a written agreement. If not, just agree by talking.

Exploring Alternatives: Five Examples

With very young children, you will want to explore alternatives as simply and briefly as possible.

Mariko, 18 months old, wants her bear, which is on the dresser. She can't reach it. Her father says, "What would happen if you pulled your stool over to the dresser and stood on it? Would you be tall enough then?" Mariko moves the stool and gets the bear. Father says, "Look what you learned, Mariko! You learned how to get your bear off the dresser."

Caitlin is 3. She has been playing with her dolls in the kitchen. It's time to fix dinner. Her parents tell her, "We can't fix supper with all your babies in here. What shall we do?" Caitlin says, "But they're sleeping. It's naptime." Dad suggests an idea, "I think they might sleep better somewhere quieter." "I know where!" says Caitlin. She begins

With very young children, explore alternatives as simply and briefly as possible.

to move the dolls to a spot behind the couch in the living room. Mom and Dad get on with supper.

Elvin is 4. He has been playing next door. His friends tell him to go home. Elvin comes home crying. His dad lets Elvin tell what happened and talk about his feelings. Then Elvin and his dad discuss what to do about the problem. Elvin suggests, "I could throw rocks at their houses! Or I could stay inside by myself all day." For each idea, his dad helps him think about the consequences. "If you throw rocks at their houses, then what will happen? How will you feel? If you stay inside all day, what will you do? How will you feel?"

Dad has guided Elvin to think about the results of his possible actions. The more he does this, the more skilled Elvin will become at choosing ideas.

Four-year-old Sofia interrupts while her mother is on the phone. Mom says, "When I'm interrupted, I feel confused. It's hard to talk to more than one person at a time. What could you do instead if you want my attention?" She and Sofia come up with three ideas:

- Before making a call, Mom can ask Sofia if she needs anything.

- Mom can tell Sofia how long the call will take. Sofia can wait patiently until the call is over. Then her mother can listen just to her.

- If Sofia has to tell Mom something, she can draw a picture of what she wants.

Mom began by exploring alternatives with her daughter. A 4-year-old may have lots of suggestions—if she feels her ideas count. Next, they'll need to choose and use an idea. Once they do this, the problem may still continue. Then a different action will be needed. Mom and Sofia will have to explore alternatives some more. They'll need to talk about a clear consequence if Sofia keeps misbehaving.

Five-year-old Julio won't accept his eight o'clock bedtime. Dad uses the five steps to talk the problem through.

1. Understand the problem.

Dad: "Julio, bedtime has gotten to be quite a problem. When you keep coming out of your room, your mom and I feel upset because we don't get to have our time alone together. How do you feel?"

Julio: "I don't like to be alone. I want to be with you guys."

Dad: "So you feel lonesome. You like it better being here with us, huh?"

2. Brainstorm ideas to find alternatives.

Dad: "Let's think of some ways we can solve this problem."

They come up with these ideas:

- Spend more time with Julio before his bedtime.
- Let Julio stay up later one night a week.
- Let Julio stay up as late as he wants.
- Let Julio listen to a tape while he goes to sleep.

3. Consider the solutions.

Dad: "Let's look at the list and see which ideas we both think are fair."

4. Choose a solution.

Julio: "I wanna stay up."
Dad: "But I worry that you won't get the sleep you need. What else might work instead?"
Julio: "Can I play a tape?"
Dad: "Okay—I'm willing to try that. Let's write an agreement."

5. Use the solution.

Together, Dad and Julio wrote this agreement:

Dad and Julio's Agreement

1. Julio will go to his bedroom at eight o'clock. He will play a story on the tape player. He will listen in bed with the lights off. He will leave his room only to use the bathroom.

2. Before Julio's bedtime, Mom and Dad will spend fifteen minutes with him. They will read a story or play a game. If Julio leaves his room after eight o'clock, he will not have that special time together the next night.

Signed: <u>Dad</u>   Julio

Dad: "Shall we use our agreement for three nights? Then we can talk about how it's working out."

What if this problem doesn't improve after a few nights? Then Dad and Julio can develop a different solution. Maybe Mom and Dad don't have much time during the day to spend with Julio. They may need to take turns spending more time with him at night. Maybe Julio is afraid of something in his room. Mom and Dad can use

Exploring alternatives can help families solve problems together.

reflective listening to find out. Julio and his parents may need to explore alternatives again. Over time, cooperating in these ways should help this family solve the problem.

Hold Family Meetings

One more good way to help young children learn to cooperate is to have regular family meetings. These meetings are not meant to be used only for solving problems. Parents and young children can use brief family meetings to:

- share good feelings
- have fun together
- make decisions about family issues
- give encouragement
- talk about problems

Family meetings are for everyone in the family. Sometimes grandparents live in the home. They need to be part of the family meetings too. They can share their feelings. They can help solve problems and make decisions. They can help plan family fun.

But a grandparent isn't in charge of the children. Discipline and final decisions are not up to them. Parenting is your job. If there is a conflict about this, talk to the grandparent. Use reflective listening. Explore alternatives. Be friendly but firm about who is responsible for parenting. You might say, "When Uriah hears two different rules, I'm afraid he'll be confused. I'm his parent. I need to be the person who sets the rules."

How much can a child take part in family meetings? It depends on the child's age.

Babies can just *be* there. Babies can take part just by being there. This will help them get used to the idea of family meetings.

Toddlers and preschoolers can handle short meetings.
Meetings will work best if they are brief and take place often. Have each meeting focus on one issue and one simple decision.

Vengh is 5. His brother Thai is 4. At a family meeting, the children and their parents talked about bathtime. Vengh and Thai didn't like bathing before supper. The family decided to try having baths before bed instead. The children wanted to take turns being first. Just before bedtime, Mom said, "It will be bathtime soon. Vengh, we agreed you'd be first tonight. Tomorrow Thai will be first. Daddy will come run your bath in ten minutes."

Meeting will work best if they are brief and take place at least once a week.

With preschoolers or slightly older children, you may want to begin more formal family meetings. It's still important to keep the meetings short and simple. And it's important that you hold the meetings regularly. This helps children learn to keep agreements over a period of time.

A Plan for a Family Meeting

1. Share good things that have happened.
2. Talk about "old business"—what happened at the last family meeting.
3. Talk about "new business"—this might be something fun people want to do together.
4. Repeat what people have agreed to.

Take the Long View

Remember, your child is learning cooperation slowly, over time. You are learning new skills too. Be patient with your child—and yourself. Through your example and practice, you can make a relationship that teaches respect and cooperation.

THIS WEEK

Decide who owns any problems that occur. Use the skills you have learned to help your child cooperate and solve problems.

POINTS TO REMEMBER

1. Cooperation means working together.

2. Children learn to cooperate slowly, over time.

3. Babies can't naturally cooperate. But they can begin to learn about cooperation.

4. Toddlers do not yet have self-control. They can *begin* to understand your messages about which behaviors are—and are not—okay.

5. Preschoolers have some self-control. They won't always understand your expectations. But their understanding is growing.

6. To decide who owns a problem, ask yourself four questions:
    *   Are my rights being disrespected?
    *   Could anybody get hurt?
    *   Are someone's belongings threatened?
    *   Is my child too young to be responsible for this problem?

    Any *one* yes answer means a parent-owned problem.

    All *four* no answers mean a child-owned problem.

7. With babies and young toddlers, parents own most of the problems.

8. With any problem, you can choose to ignore it, use reflective listening, use an I-message, give a choice, set a limit, or explore alternatives.

9. To explore alternatives, follow these five steps:
    1. Understand the problem.
    2. Brainstorm ideas to find alternatives.
    3. Consider the solutions.
    4. Choose a solution.
    5. Use the solution.

10. Regular family meetings can build cooperation. With your young child, keep these meetings brief.

JUST FOR YOU

Solving Adult Problems

Sometimes you have conflicts with other adults. You can explore alternatives then too. Follow these steps:

1. Understand the problem.
2. Brainstorm ideas to find alternatives.
3. Discuss the ideas. Consider the suggested solutions.
4. Choose an idea.
5. Use the idea. Set a time to talk about how the idea is working.

Keep these ideas in mind:*

- **Stay respectful.** Avoid fighting or giving in. Use reflective listening and I-messages.

- **Talk about the real problem.** Many times the real issue is who's right or what's fair. You can say: "It seems like we're both trying to prove who's right. I wonder how that will help us solve the problem."

- **Agree not to fight.** In a conflict, you have "agreed" to fight. To change this agreement, change your own behavior. Be willing to compromise.

- **Invite each person to help make a decision.** An agreement comes when people *work together* to solve a problem. What if this doesn't happen? Say what *you* will do: "Since we aren't able to talk through this problem, I'm going to (say what you will do).

In problems with another adult, think about how you can explore alternatives. How will you start the discussion? Make an effort to work on the problem together.

---

*Rudolf Dreikurs and Loren Grey, *A Parent's Guide to Child Discipline* (New York: Hawthorn, 1970), pp. 42-43.

Chart 5

WHO OWNS THE PROBLEM?

Age	What happens?	Who owns the problem?	What can parent say/do?
Infants	Usually best to assume that parent owns problem. Crying may mean child is hungry, wet, tired, sick.		
Toddlers	Child wants cookie. Parents says no. Child throws tantrum.	Child	1. *Use reflective listening:* "I see you're very angry about not getting a cookie." 2. *Offer a choice:* "You may have a banana or an apple." 3. *Ignore tantrum* if child persists.
	Child refuses to be buckled into car seat.	Parent	Child *must* be buckled in for safety: "You don't like the car seat. But to be safe, you must be buckled in."
Preschoolers	Two children fight over toy.	Children	1. *Help them explore alternatives:* "You both want to play with the toy. Can you think of a way to share it?" 2. If they don't cooperate but don't hit, *let them work it out on their own.* 3. If children hit or you are bothered by arguing, *separate or send one child home.*
	Child spills juice.	Child	Let child clean up spill. Help if necessary.
	Child refuses to go to doctor.	Parent	Parent gives choice: "You can walk into the doctor's office, or I can carry you. You decide."

CHAPTER SIX

Young Children

You have looked at many ways to help your child become more co-operative and responsible. For example, setting expectations that are positive and realistic promotes cooperation. Using respect and encouragement to help your child belong helps develop responsibility. Using reflective listening and I-messages helps you talk about feelings and problems. All of these are part of an effective discipline system.

Are Discipline and Punishment the Same Thing?

Some people think that *discipline* means *punishment*. Discipline and punishment are *not* the same thing. Many of us grew up with parents who used rewards and punishment to control our behavior. In Chapter 1, we talked about what children learn from these methods:

- Rewards teach children to get something—not to cooperate.

- Punishment teaches children to resent and fear us. This can lower self-esteem. It can hurt the relationship we want to have.

What Is Punishment?

Punishment includes many things.

Threats, yelling, and put-downs. Sometimes the threats are carried out, sometimes not, Sometimes yelling makes things worse. If

Here's what you will learn . . .

- Discipline and punishment are not the same thing.

- The goal of discipline is to teach your child self-discipline.

- You can give your child choices within limits.

- Disciplining with respect and consistency is possible.

we yell a lot, children may start to pay attention *only* when we shout. Put-downs aren't helpful either.

Taking things away. Often parents take things away from children as a punishment. Many times what is taken away has nothing to do with what the child did. The child does not learn.

Spanking and hitting. Spanking shows children that hitting is a way to solve a problem. It hurts. Children may become afraid. Often, a parent hits a child out of anger. Later on, the parent may feel guilty. Spanking children also teaches them that if you're bigger, you can get your way by hitting. Bullies often believe this.

What Is Discipline?

Discipline is not a single act or statement. It is a process. Both learning *to* discipline and learning *from* it take time.

The goal of discipline is to teach children *self*-discipline. It is to guide children to be responsible and to cooperate. When children misbehave, we use discipline to help them choose a better way to behave.

How Can I Discipline My Child?

Children respond to respect and positive expectations. There are many positive, respectful ways to discipline. You can:

- **D**istract the child.
- **I**gnore misbehavior.
- **S**tructure the environment.
- **C**ontrol the situation, not the child.
- **I**nvolve the child.
- **P**lan time for loving.
- **L**et go.
- **I**ncrease your consistency.
- **N**otice positive behavior.
- **E**xcuse the child with a time-out.

Some methods will work better for you than others. In choosing discipline, thinking about your child's age and stage of development is important. Another element in effective discipline is *your belief* that the idea will work.

Let's look more closely at each way to discipline.

Discipline and punishment are not the same thing.

Distract the Child

Sheryl is 13 months old. She scoots toward the flower vase in the corner. "Sheryl!" her mom calls firmly. Sheryl pauses and looks at her mom. Then Mom picks Sheryl up in a friendly way. She takes her to a toy in the other corner of the room.

Sheryl's mother *distracts* her child. First she calls Sheryl's name to get her attention. Then she steers Sheryl to another part of the room. She focuses Sheryl's attention on something else. Mom does all this in a friendly way.

Taking action and talking less help avoid a struggle for attention or power. What else can Sheryl's mom do?

- She can move Sheryl to a different room to play.

- She can give Sheryl something else to play with.

Distraction works especially well with babies. If your 4 month old pulls on your ear, give your baby something else to play with!

Ignore Misbehavior

Misha is 3. He wants a glass of juice. In the past, his dad has explained that he will give Misha what he wants if he says "please." But today Misha doesn't say "please." He whines for juice. Paying no attention, Dad goes on fixing supper.

Misha whines again. Then he remembers why he isn't getting what he wants. He asks for juice again. This time he says "please" in a pleasant voice. Dad says, "I'd be happy to get you juice. You asked me in a respectful way."

Misha's father has *ignored* Misha's misbehavior. Ignoring is a skill that can be helpful for many problem behaviors: showing off, sulking, whining, mild crying, temper tantrums, power plays, interrupting, begging for treats, and insults.

Some things can't be ignored. If your child is hurting someone or is in danger, you can't ignore the behavior.

Watch your body language. Think about what your face and body tell your child. If you say nothing but look angry, you aren't really ignoring the behavior. Your child sees this. Keep in mind, too, that most children don't give up easily. The behavior may get worse for a while. Concentrate on what you are doing. Keep your face calm. Your patience will usually pay off.

Both learning to discipline and learning from it take time.

Young children need lots of "hands-on" experiences.

Structure the Environment

A dish of candy sits on Grandma's table. Two-year-old Bonnie takes a piece. Grandma tells Bonnie that one piece is all she may have. Then Grandma puts the dish in the cupboard.

Bonnie's grandma is *structuring the environment.* She knows Bonnie will want more candy. By putting it out of reach, she helps Bonnie forget about the candy. Grandma could also use a safety gate to close off the room. She could place Bonnie in a playpen for a short while. This would keep Bonnie safe if Grandma had something else she needed to do quickly.

"Hands-On"

Young children need to explore. This is how they learn. They need to have lots of "hands-on" experiences. Structuring the environment helps us say "Hands off!" less often.

Structuring the environment has other names: *childproofing* or *babyproofing.* As soon as babies can move around on their own, it's time to childproof your home. You can't remove every single danger or put everything out of reach. But you can make your home much safer.

You can also structure by what the child *can* do. Place within easy reach things the child *may* touch and use. This will help give your child a hands-on experience. It will make it easier for you to watch your child. Keeping your child—and your special things—safe will be easier.

"Mine" and "Yours"

Toddlers are learning about "my" and "mine." At the same time, you are teaching your child to leave certain things alone. As you do, you help your child begin to learn the difference between "mine" and "yours."

Chuck is 2 1/2. Dad shows Chuck a special piece of driftwood. "This is mine," he says to his son. "Please ask before you touch it." Then he points to Chuck's stuffed lion. He says, "Rex is yours. May I hold him?" Chuck's dad repeats this process from time to time. Chuck is learning about ownership.

Over time, your child will learn to respect what belongs to you. As this happens, gradually start to leave more of your things around. Of course, every child will make mistakes! Your child learns self-control and respect for what belongs to others by reasonable experiences.

Routines

Following routines is another way to structure the environment. There are three important times to follow routines: in the morning, at mealtimes, and at bedtime. Routines give your child limits. *Children need limits.* Limits help children know what to expect. Your routine may not match your neighbor's That's okay. What's important is that you set a routine and stick to it most of the time.

Diego is 3. In his home, breakfast comes after dressing. Lunch, snacks, and supper are eaten at about the same time each day. A bath and a story come before bedtime.

Control the Situation, Not the Child

Parents often think they must control their children. They fear that if they do not, their children will control *them.* But children want—and need—to feel some control too. Having some positive control helps children become independent and confident.

How can you give your child this positive control? *Control the situation—not the child.* You do this by setting limits and giving choices.

Set Limits

Instead of giving orders, set limits. Structuring the environment sets limits. The child is free to explore most spaces and things. If the child breaks something or does something dangerous, use these ideas:

- Distract the child.

- Remove the item that is off limits.

- Use a door or gate so the child has boundaries.

- Remove the child, if necessary.

Give Choices

You can give your older toddler or preschooler choices within limits you create. The limits give you some control. Having choices gives your child some control:

- "You may play quietly while I'm on the phone, or you may leave the room. You decide."

- "Which of these toys would you like to take to Grandpa's?"

- "How many peas would you like—this many, or this many?"

- "Would you like to wear your red jammies to bed, or your blue ones?"

Children learn more about cooperation when they feel that you value their wishes.

Involve the Child

By giving young children choices, we *involve* them in the discipline process. This helps them build independence and cooperation.

When you offer a choice, your child may say, "No, I want *this!*" Then you might say, "That's not one of the choices."

Natural and Logical Consequences

When you need to correct your child's behavior, you can use a *consequence*. A consequence results from a child's choice.

Natural consequences just happen. For example, a child who refuses to eat lunch gets hungry. A tired child becomes cranky.

Logical consequences don't *just* happen. Parents create logical consequences.

Terrence is 3. He rides his trike into Kristen, on purpose. Logical consequences follow. Terrence's mom may take away Terrence's trike-riding privileges for a while. She may say, "I see you're not ready to use your bike the right way."

Many situations don't have natural consequences. Also, many natural consequences aren't safe. Then you will need to create a logical consequence.

Blia is 2 1/2. Her dad knows he can't let her run into the street to learn the danger of being hit by a car! So Dad sets up a logical consequence. He says, "Blia, the street's not for playing. You could get hurt by a car. You may play in the yard or inside—you decide. If you go near the street, I'll know you've decided to come inside for a while."

What if Blia decides to go in the street? Then Dad knows she has made a choice: to go inside for a while. A little later, Dad can give her another chance. If Blia goes back near the street, she's chosen to play inside again. This time Dad will need to keep her inside a little longer. In this way, Blia will learn the limits.

How Is a Consequence Different From Punishment?

Here are some ways consequences are different from punishment:

- They show respect for both you and your child.

- They fit the misbehavior.

- They are for bad choices—not bad children.

- They are about now—not the past.

- They are firm and friendly.
- They allow choice within limits.

Consequences Show Respect

Consequences show respect—for *both* you and your child.

You are talking with another adult. Your child, James, comes into the room to play. His play becomes noisy. You don't yell, "Be quiet, or get out of here!" You say, "James, we are trying to talk. Either play quietly or go to another room to play."

Consequences "Fit"

Consequences make sense. They fit the misbehavior.

You tell your 3 year old where she may ride her trike. She rides outside the boundaries. You don't put her to bed early. Bedtime has nothing to do with trike riding. Instead, you give her a choice. You say, "You may ride where I showed you, or put the trike away and do something else for a while."

Consequences Are About Behavior

Consequences are for bad choices—not "bad" children. You may have heard the phrase, "Separate the deed from the doer." Consequences help you do this. It is the misbehavior—not the child—that needs to be fixed! Consequences tell your child, "I don't like what you're doing, but I still love you."

Your preschooler gets angry and throws food on the floor on purpose. You don't yell at him or spank him. You simply assume he has finished eating. You might say, "I see you've finished. Our next meal will be . . ." Then you excuse him from the table.

Consequences Are About Now

Consequences are about now—not the past.

Your child wants to ask a friend over to play. Last time the friend came to play, the children fought. You don't say, "No! All you two ever do is fight!" You say, "You can invite Sam over if you can cooperate and are willing to play nicely. If there's fighting, Sam will have to go home."

Here you have focused on what the children will do *now*—not what they've done in the past. You've also explained what you mean by *cooperation*. This gives your child a chance to hear and learn what cooperation is.

Consequences Are Firm and Friendly

Consequences are firm and friendly. They show respect and caring.

Consequences tell your child, "I don't like what you're doing, but I still love you."

It's bedtime for your 2 1/2 year old. You don't say, "Get to bed quick, or else!" Instead, you say, "You need to go to bed now. Would you like to walk to your room, or would it be fun to be carried?"

Babies and Consequences

In most cases, babies are too young for logical consequences. Children this young aren't ready to think logically. Of course, there will be problems with babies' behavior. And there will be consequences.

Suppose an infant pokes her father in the nose. He may hold her hand or place her on the floor. That way he won't be poked again. But he can't assume that a 1 year old <u>understands</u> the consequences of her behavior. The child <u>does</u> learn from the experience what to do or not to do. But this learning may not be long-term.

Consequences Allow Choice

With a choice, the child has some control.

You tell your 2 year old, "You may play with the dog if you touch her gently. If you hit her, you will have to play with something else."

Guidelines for Using Logical Consequences

Here are some ways to make consequences effective.

Accept the Choice

When your child decides, let the decision stand—for the moment. Later, offer your child another chance to cooperate.

Damita is 5. She eats granola in the family room and leaves crumbs all over. The next time she has a snack, she's allowed to eat it in the kitchen—not the family room. After that, she can try again.

Some children have trouble deciding. They may not know what they want. They might want you to decide for them. When this happens, limit the child's time to make a choice.

Children may be indecisive. Parents can help by letting the choice stand.

Melissa is 3. Her stepmom offers her a choice of snacks. Melissa has trouble choosing. "Think about it, Melissa," her stepmom says. "Then let me know what you decide."

Ten minutes later, Melissa comes and says, "I still can't pick." Her stepmom says, "Okay. I'll set the buzzer on the stove for ten minutes. You decide by then." "But what if I still can't pick?" Melissa asks. With a friendly tone of voice, Melissa's stepmom says, "If you can't pick by then, I'll know you have decided you don't want a snack."

Add Time for Repeated Misbehavior

Each time the same misbehavior occurs, increase the amount of time for the consequence.

On her second chance, Damita again leaves a mess in the family room. As she and her family have agreed, she now may not eat in the family room for the next two snacktimes.

Use Respectful Words

When giving a choice, state the possibilities in a friendly and helpful tone. One way is to say: "You may _____ or _____. You decide."

- "You may settle down, or you may leave the room. You decide."

- "You can play nicely with Gerri or come for a walk with Daddy. You decide."

Another way to give a choice is to say, "You may _____ if you _____."

- "You may play with the baby if you don't pinch him."

- "You can ride on my shoulders if you sit still."

Another way is simply to tell your child what *you* will do:

- "I'll help you when you ask me nicely."

- "If you're not dressed when the timer goes off, you've decided to go to child care in your pajamas."

Respect the Choice

Your child may choose some consequences as a way to test you. The child wants to see if you mean what you say.

When this happens, respect your child's choice. Simply say, "I see you've decided. You can try again tomorrow." Keep your voice, face, and body matter-of-fact.

Talk Less, Act More

Children quit listening when parents talk too much. The best time for talk is when you and your child are on friendly terms. When you

Children quit listening when parents talk too much.

Yelling, nagging, or making threats turn a consequence into punishment.

use consequences, talk as little as possible as you follow through with action.

Make It Clear When There *Isn't* a Choice

Lots of times parents will offer a choice they don't really mean. If there really *is* no choice, don't hint that there is. This just creates more problems. Instead, be clear about what you expect.

It's time for Freda to come in from playing. Her mom doesn't ask, "Do you want to come in now, Freda?" Mom knows she'll probably get a no! Instead, Mom says, "It's time to come in now."

What if Freda says, "Not yet. I wanna play some more." Mom can give Freda a choice of how she wants to come in: "Do you want to come in on your own, or shall I help you?" Then Mom can watch what Freda does. She can act on Freda's decision.

Stay Calm

Yelling, nagging, or making threats turn a consequence into punishment. Keep calm. Be both kind and firm. Show respect for yourself and your child.

Practicing in front of a mirror might help you. Watch your face and body. Listen to your tone of voice. This will help you be ready for the unexpected.

Plan Time for Loving

Your child needs your attention. Spending some special time with your child each day is important. Make this part of your routine. Play, cuddle, and enjoy each other. Your child needs this for emotional development. Your relationship needs it too. It can also help prevent behavior problems.

Odina is 2. Every night before bed, her mother rocks Odina and sings to her. This has become a real sharing time. Odina sings along and asks for favorite songs. This loving routine gives Mother and Odina fifteen to twenty minutes of close time each day. Also it builds their relationship and helps Odina settle down for the night.

Sef is 4. He and his father are early risers. In the morning, they walk the dog together before Father leaves for work. The morning walk gives Father and Sef regular time together. It's also a nice start to their day!

Let Go

Your child is growing and learning to cooperate. You can show that you see this. You can build your child's confidence. How? By learning to *let go* and be less controlling.

Of course, children need protection. But too much protection is not good. You need to find a balance:

- A father can watch a crawling baby explore in the grass. He doesn't need to be right beside her every second.

- A mother can watch from nearby while her 2-year old greets a friendly dog on a leash.

- A parent can allow a 5 year old to learn to ride a bike. The child will take some tumbles in the process.

Giving in or giving orders won't help us let go. Remember, children need choices within limits. Ask yourself, "Will this behavior help my child learn to cooperate with others?" If the answer is no, then you'll want to set limits on the behavior.

Letting go is a process. Beginning when our children are very young, it continues over many years. As our children show respectful behavior, we let go more and more.

Letting go is a process. It continues over many years.

Increase Your Consistency

With discipline, *consistency* is important. You treat the same behavior in the same way—no matter where or when. Of course, no parent is perfect. You won't always be consistent. Your goal is to increase your consistency. The more consistent you are, the more effective your discipline will be.

Be Consistent in Public

Being consistent is not always easy. But it's worth the effort. Then your child will know the limits and what to expect.

You and your preschooler are going shopping. Before you go, you say, "We won't be buying toys today. We need some things for our home." At the store, your child wants a toy he has seen on television. He starts to beg. You place him beside you, ignore the fussing, and go on with your shopping. Finally, you say, "If you keep fussing, then you've decided to go home."

Your child fusses more and more. You stop shopping and head home. You stay respectful. You tell your child, "I see you've decided to come home."

Restaurants can be a problem too. Choose a family restaurant that serves food your child likes. Talk about what the child will order ahead of time: "Will you order a cheeseburger, or chicken nuggets?"

Let your child bring along a small toy. Stick to your usual behavior rules. If the child misbehaves, the child's meal is over. You or another adult can take the child outside. Wait there for the others to finish eating. Sometimes this isn't possible. Then you may have to end your own meal as well. It's unpleasant for you, but your child learns the limits.

For babies and toddlers, running errands and eating out can be stressful. If possible, find a way to do the errands by yourself. If it's not possible, plan to make errands easier. Start by making sure your child is fed and rested. While you run errands, find ways to help your child take part and enjoy it:

- At the post office, let your child drop the letters into the slot.

- At the grocery store, ask your child the names of fruits and vegetables.

Don't Worry About What Others Think

Visiting others and having company over can be stressful. A baby may become fussier than usual. A toddler may lose some self-control. Understanding this can help you stay consistent.

Children have minds of their own. They won't always act as we wish they would.

Relatives and friends may say:

- "Oh, let her have another cookie!"

- "It's okay—he's not bothering me."

This can be challenging. Stay calm and friendly, but firm. Say to the adult, "Thanks for your patience. But two cookies are enough." If the fussing continues, you may have to leave or take your child out of the room.

It's not easy to stand firm when another parent questions you. But the message to your child is a clear one. Your child sees that your limits are consistent. You are building respect.

Sometimes parents are embarrassed when a child misbehaves. They think it shows that they are weak. But children have minds of their own. They won't always act as we wish they would. When they don't it's not always because of us.

When Other Children Come to Play

When playmates visit, discipline problems often occur. Don't accept your child's misbehavior just because another child is visiting. Let your discipline be the same.

Children who visit your home also need to know your discipline rules. Explain them. Follow through if problems occur. At first, children may test you. Stay firm and friendly. Children will see that you mean what you say. Then they will probably be more willing to cooperate. If not, you may need to end the visit and send the guest home.

When Rules Are Different

Different homes have different rules. Help your child understand this: "At home, it's okay for you to play in my bedroom. But at Molly's, you play only where Molly's mother wants you to."

Notice Positive Behavior

Limits are necessary. Still, we can balance limits with positive words and actions. When you *notice positive behavior*, you can say yes to your child more than you say no. This is because you talk about what is positive and say nothing about what *isn't*.

Notice when your child cooperates with others: "Robbie, it looks like you and Ramón are enjoying playing together." This is good for your child's self-esteem. It can also help encourage more positive behavior.

Use a time-out as a last resort—to help your child or you gain control.

Excuse the Child With a Time-Out

Time-out can help a toddler or preschooler regain self-control. It can give a child time to calm down. Here is a word of caution, though: Use a time-out as a *last resort*—when other discipline methods haven't worked. A time-out is appropriate only for *very disruptive behaviors*, such as:

- temper tantrums
- constant interruptions
- hitting or biting

The Purpose of a Time-Out

A time-out has two purposes:

- to teach a child that she or he must learn to control behavior if the child wants to be around others
- to give *you* a chance to keep control of your own behavior and feelings

Guidelines for Using Time-Out

Here are some ways to make time-out effective.

1. **Choose a place for the time-out.** The spot for time-out needs to be away from people. You might use the child's bedroom, though some parents worry about doing this. They are afraid it will cause the child to dislike the bedroom. By staying matter-of-fact and keeping your purpose in mind, time-out in the bedroom won't seem like punishment. It will simply give your child and you some quiet space. If you feel the child will hurt or break something, put the item out of reach ahead of time.

   Some parents fear their child will kick the door or wall. Walls and doors can be repaired much more easily than self-esteem!

2. **Explain the rules.** Children need to know the rules of the time-out. When possible, talk about this *before* a problem arises. You might say, "When your behavior tells me you're not ready to be with other people, I'll know you need a time-out." Explain that you'll set a timer or use another signal. When the child hears the buzzer, the time-out is over—if the child is ready to settle down.

3. **Plan the length of time.** One or two minutes is plenty for a first time-out. Add a minute for each new time-out. An easy guideline is *no more than* one minute for each year of a child's

Children learn best when they are having fun.

age. This means that a 3 year old's time-out will never last more than three minutes. A 5 year old's will never be longer than five minutes.

Some children are able to decide on their own when they're ready to come out. Then you won't need the timer. Tell your child: "You may come out when you are ready to calm down." In this way, your child will be developing self-control.

4. **Don't lock the door.** Locking the door can be dangerous. It can also leave the child feeling trapped and afraid. True, with an unlocked door, the child may come out of the room before the time limit. If this happens, firmly but kindly return the child to the room.

5. **Allow the child to play.** It's okay if the child plays during time-out. This shows that the child has regained some control. Remember, it's a time-out, not a punishment.

6. **When a time-out is over, it's over.** Don't discuss the time-out. That would call attention to the behavior you want to stop.

How Can I Avoid Discipline Problems?

We can't avoid all problem behaviors. But we can reduce them. How? By taking the time to teach children skills they need so they can cooperate.

When teaching any skill, make sure your child is interested. Find a time that's pleasant for both of you. If *either* of you gets tired or bored, stop. Try it again some other time.

Children learn best when they are having fun.

Moira said to her son Danny, "Let's play a game—a dressing game. I'll help you learn to dress yourself." First, Moira had Danny put his clothes on backward. Looking in the mirror, they laughed together. Moira said, "That's how we would dress if we walked backward!"

Next, Moira helped Danny put on one thing—his shirt—correctly. Danny looked at that in the mirror. Then Moira said, "Now you choose what to put on next." Danny chose his shoe. He put it on the right foot. He looked in the mirror and said, "Oh-oh. I forgot my sock." Moira said, "So you did! What can you do?" Danny took off his shoe and put on his sock. When his foot got stuck in the shoe, Moira showed him how to pull at the back of the shoe and put his heel inside.

This took quite a while. But Danny and Moira both had a good time. And Danny learned many things that he remembered the next time.

What if Danny decided to wear his shirt backward? His mom might say, "I see you've decided it's fun to dress backward!" Or she could say, "It's fun to be silly—but we need to dress right today."

Discipline Is Teaching

Your child is learning many skills. You are learning too. Learning effective discipline takes time—for both you and your child. Keep in mind the purpose of discipline: to teach your child *self*-discipline.

Be patient. Have realistic expectations for yourself. Stay respectful. Your child will see the respect you have for both of you.

THIS WEEK

Use some of the discipline methods in this chapter. As you do, think about your child's age and stage of development. Write down specific incidents. Identify what you did that was most effective.

Encouragement
STEP

Your beliefs and expectations influence your child. You believe your child deserves respect and is capable. Communicate these beliefs to your child! When you do, your child will feel respected and capable. Then he or she is likely to act more respectful and capable.

To communicate that you believe in your child:

- Focus on your child's interests.

- Cooperate with your child instead of competing.

- Speak to your child respectfully.

- Notice your child's special talents and qualities.

- Value what is unique about your child.

Look for ways to communicate that you believe in your child.

POINTS TO REMEMBER

1. Discipline and punishment are not the same thing.

2. In choosing a way to discipline, you need to consider your child's age and stage of development.

3. Choose from these methods of discipline:
   - **D**istract the child.
   - **I**gnore misbehavior.
   - **S**tructure the environment.
   - **C**ontrol the situation, not the child.
   - **I**nvolve the child.
   - **P**lan time for loving.
   - **L**et go.
   - **I**ncrease your consistency.
   - **N**otice positive behavior.
   - **E**xcuse the child with a time-out.

4. Instead of giving orders, set limits and give choices. Limits give you some control; choices give your child some control.

5. A consequence is what happens because of a choice the child makes. Consequences are a way to set limits and give choices. Consequences:
   - show respect for you and your child
   - fit the misbehavior
   - are for bad choices, not bad children
   - are about now, not the past
   - are firm and friendly
   - allow choice

6. Some guidelines for using consequences are:
   - Accept the choice.
   - Add time for repeated misbehavior.
   - Use respectful words.
   - Respect the choice.
   - Talk less, act more.
   - Make it clear when there *isn't* a choice.
   - Stay calm.

Continued on next page.

7. Your child needs to have special time with you every day. This is good for your relationship. And it can help prevent behavior problems.

8. Use a time-out as a last resort, when other methods haven't worked. The purpose of a time-out is to help your child and you gain control.

9. Choose a relaxed time to teach skills, and make the training fun.

JUST FOR YOU

The Rights of Parents and Children

Parents and children have rights. Centering your life on your children is not fair to you or your child.

As a parent, you have the right to:

- friendships

- privacy

- time for yourself

- respect for your belongings

- a life apart from your child

Your child has the right to:

- be raised in a safe and loving home

- friendships outside the family

- privacy

- respect for belongings

These rights can be summed up in the word *respect.*

This week, look for ways to keep your rights. What will you do to show respect for your child's rights?

Chart 6

*USING LOGICAL CONSEQUENCES**

Infants	With babies, assume problem behavior is not misbehavior. Check to see if child is hungry, tired, sick, or wet. Understand baby's needs and abilities. Make a safe area of hands-–on activities. Once baby can move around, child-proofing is a must.
Toddlers/Preschoolers	Hands-on activities are important for these children too. Childproofing is still needed. Give clear guidelines and limits.

What does child do?	What can you do?
Doesn't come to meal when called.	**Toddler:** Be matter-of-fact. Bring child to table. If child has tantrum, move child to safe place. Don't feed again until usual snacktime. **Preschooler:** Set timer. If child not at table when timer goes off, don't feed. Wait until usual snacktime.
Doesn't pick up toys.	Delay next activity until toys are picked up. Help or suggest one step at a time. The younger the child, the smaller each task/step should be.
Demands attention.	Ignore child or leave room.
Upsets play group activity.	Have child leave area.
Is not careful in handling object.	Show careful use. If child misuses again, deny use for a while.
Loses or destroys own toy.	Make sure toy fits child's age. Guide child to put toy away. Show how to use. Once child understands, do not replace toy.
Misbehaves in store or other public place.	Leave store with child or do not take child on next trip.
Makes mess eating away from table.	**Toddler:** Toddlers can't help being messy. Avoid trouble by not giving food at places other than table. **Preschooler:** Don't allow food away from table if child makes mess.
Doesn't feed pet.	**Toddler:** Too young to remember every day. Tell child each time pet is to be fed. If no cooperation, do not feed child until pet is fed. **Preschooler:** May need to remind child from time to time. If no cooperation, do not feed child until pet is fed.
Demands help.	Wait to help until child asks respectfully. If child has tantrum, help child calm down, then discuss.

*Adapted from Jerrold I. Gilbert, "Logical Consequences: A New Classification." *Individual Psychology 42*, #2 (June 1986): pp. 243-54.

CHAPTER SEVEN

Young Children's
Social
and **Emotional**
Development

Young children are developing in many ways. Their bodies are growing. A healthy diet, rest, and physical activity help them grow. Their minds are developing. They learn through activities that fit their age, interests, and abilities. Children are also developing in two other important ways:

emotionally—in their feelings and how they handle them

socially—in the ways they relate to other people

Your child needs your help to develop emotionally and socially. In this chapter, you will learn some ways to give this help. One of the most important things you can do is show *empathy*. This means you can see, understand, and accept your child's feelings. By showing empathy, you teach your child to accept others. You help your child's emotional and social development when you teach:

- being able to see another person's point of view
- caring about another person's feelings
- listening to another person

Understanding Emotional Development

Children grow emotionally at different rates. And they may handle an emotion differently as they grow.

Here's what you will learn . . .

- **Your child can learn healthy ways to share feelings.**
- **You can set limits and encourage independence.**
- **You can help your child and yourself develop courage to meet challenges.**

Soor is 3. Today she feels happy and sure of herself. She is coming home from the park with her dad. A neighbor's dog barks and runs to greet them. Soor says to her dad, "Doggie won't hurt us."

The next day, Soor has a bad afternoon. She feels cranky and unsure of herself. She and her dad take the same walk home. This time, she is scared when the dog comes toward her. She clings to her dad. He says, "It's all right, Soor. You feel afraid. But the dog is only saying hello."

Ways to Help Your Child Share Feelings

You can help your children learn healthy ways to share feelings.

Share your own feelings. Remember the importance of what you do and say. Show your feelings in ways you'd want your child to show his or hers. If you feel happy, smile and say you are happy. If you want your child to handle anger without exploding, show how to do that too.

Listen and talk about feelings. Be aware of your child's *feelings*. Show clearly that you see and understand them: "I hear the thunder too. It sounds scary." Here are other ways to show understanding:

- **Use reflective listening:** "You feel unhappy." "You seem confused."

- **Recognize your child's uniqueness:** "You like to sing while you play with your blocks."

- **Fix any breaks in your relationship.** For example, when you've been angry, you might say: "I apologize for being so angry. Let's talk about it."

- **Help your child see that it's normal to feel confused.** It's okay to be angry with someone you love. "Sometimes you like to play with your brother, but not when he hits."

Play with your child. Play gives you a chance to talk about feelings your child may be avoiding. You can use puppets, dolls, and stuffed animals.

Four-year-old Anika's grandma died. Her mom was very sad. Over the next few weeks, Anika started to misbehave more and more often. One afternoon, Anika's dad asked her to get her dolls so they could play together. "I wonder if your dolly has a grandma," he said to Anika. "Dolly's grandma died," Anika said.

As they played, Anika told her dad that "Dolly" was upset to see her mother cry so much. Dad also learned that "Dolly" thought her mother had forgotten about her. Through play, Dad learned about what Anika was feeling. He was able to begin to help her talk about and understand her feelings.

Play is a way to talk about feelings.

Set appropriate limits. Even when you show understanding, you need to set limits: "I see you're angry because Eli broke your toy. But people aren't for hitting. Come play over here until you're not so angry."

Allow comfort objects. One way infants and small children deal with their feelings is by depending on objects. They may use a stuffed animal or special blanket to comfort themselves when they are tired or afraid. Caring for a doll, a teddy bear, or a blanket now may help a child love other people later.

Feelings and Misbehavior

Young children don't outgrow the need to have us understand their feelings. With each year, it becomes more likely that *at times* they will begin to use feelings to get attention or power. Be sensitive to this and set limits kindly and firmly.

Craig is 4. He wants some cookies. Dad knows Craig ate lunch and had a good snack a little while ago. Supper will be ready soon, so Dad says, "It's too close to supper." Craig whines, "I'm hungry." Next he yells, "I want cookies! Give me some!" He throws a fit. Finally, Dad can't take any more and sends Craig to his room.

Craig's goal is more than cookies—it's become power. He uses extreme feelings—a temper tantrum—to try to reach that goal.

Dad's response in fact has brought on more of the misbehavior he wants to stop!

Understanding that his son wants power can help Dad. He can decide to bow out of the power struggle. He can ignore Craig's whining and yelling. If he finally needs to take Craig from the room, he can do it calmly and matter-of-factly: "I see you've decided not to stay in the kitchen, Craig. You may come back when you're ready to cooperate."

Emotional Challenges

You face many challenges when dealing with your child's feelings. Let's look at a few of the most common that most parents of young children face.

Crying

We want to comfort crying children. But also be aware that tears and cries can become powerful tools. Young children have trouble putting their feelings into words. So they often express some feelings by crying. Children can learn to use crying to get attention or to pull a parent into a power struggle. Sometimes crying can "trap" parents. Then parents may give in to a child's demands. Or they may get angry and yell or hit. They might even feel guilty.

Kordie is 3. She likes her stepmom to build blocks with her. Lately, when it's time to put the blocks away for bed, Kordie cries. She yells, "No—I want to play more!" Her stepmom feels irritated. She feels guilty too. She works all day, so she doesn't have a lot of time to spend with Kordie. Playing longer stops the crying—but only until Kordie's stepmom again says it's time to quit.

Kordie has found a sure way to keep her stepmom's attention. But letting Kordie get power this way isn't helping her learn to deal with her feelings. Kordie's stepmom would be wise to say, "You're mad that we have to quit now. But it's bedtime." Then she can matter-of-factly help Kordie pick up the blocks and get ready for bed. This stepmom can also look for ways to use Kordie's desire for power in a positive way. She might ask Kordie to help set the table. She might notice when Kordie "reads" to her baby brother.

Crying *isn't* always misbehavior. How can you tell? Look carefully at the situation. Notice your own feelings and responses. Doing this will help you avoid letting your toddler or preschooler use crying for a negative goal.

Sadness

In the same way they use crying, older toddlers and preschoolers can at times use sadness to gain attention or demonstrate power. The lower lip comes out. The head goes down. We can usually tell if a child is pouting to get special treatment.

More often, though, sadness in a child is a cry for help. Such a cry cannot be ignored. Sadness comes in response to a loss—the loss of a friend, the death of a pet. It can happen every day with some other major disappointment. Help your child talk about such an experience. Listen to your child's feelings. Use reflective listening. Help your child know you hear and understand.

Share Your Own Grief

Grief and loss are part of life. When someone close to you dies, you may feel like withdrawing from your child to be alone. This is natural. But do what you can to share your feelings with your child. It helps your child learn about death from you. It also helps your child to see and learn about your feelings of sorrow. If you aren't able to share feelings, ask another adult to talk and listen to your child.

If a parent, grandparent, or relative dies, share your feelings with your child. Be open. This will help you *and* your child. As time passes, you will become ready to shift the focus away from sadness. Then you and your child can share happy memories about the person who has died.

Crying sometimes can be misbehavior.

Watch for Signs of Depression

When a child is sad and cries, this is usually a healthy emotional response. But sometimes sadness may hide other feelings. Loneliness, anger, or depression may all appear on the surface to be sadness. It is important to determine why a child is sad. A depressed child may show these signs:

- a loss of energy

- withdrawal

- feelings of hopelessness

- no attempt to express feelings

Helping When Your Child Feels Sad

When your child is sad or depressed, what can you do?

1. **Empathize.** Do not make light of the feelings. Don't ignore them. Listen and understand. This will help your child come to understand the feelings.

2. **Encourage your child.** Find ways for the child to do enjoyable things and experience success. Focus on and recognize any positive behavior.

3. **Show your care and support.** Do not dig for deep-seated reasons. Help your child feel protected and cared for.

When a child is sad for a long time, you will want to get some help. Talk to your child's doctor or to a professional counselor.

Jealousy

Jealousy is often especially strong for children ages 18 months to 3 1/2 years. We can't totally get rid of jealousy in children. Just the same, we can help make the jealousy less intense. How? By helping children understand jealous feelings:

- "Are you feeling angry because Daddy has to feed the baby now?"

- "You seem sad when Rory goes to school and you don't."

When There's a New Baby

Here are some ideas for dealing with a child's jealousy about a new baby:

- Make sure the child knows ahead of time that a new sister or brother will be coming.

- Spend special time with your toddler or preschooler. The baby will take most of your time. But your older child still needs your time and attention.

- Have the older child help with the baby. A young child can bring diapers or help feed the baby.

- Don't leave a jealous toddler alone with a new baby. A jealous child may hug the baby too tightly. He or she may poke or hit the baby.

- A jealous child may decide to be a baby again. The child may increase thumb sucking, talk "baby" talk, be cranky, make demands, or cling to you. Reassurance from you can help when a child is jealous of a newborn.

- Have realistic expectations. A new baby's arrival doesn't mean your toddler or preschooler is no longer a young child.

Ask an older child to help you with a new baby.

Fears

Children often express fear to let us know they need help. T. Berry Brazelton, a well-known children's doctor, offers these suggestions:

- Accept fears as normal.

- Understand why your child is fearful.

- Maintain limits.

- Help your child find outlets for feelings.

Let's look at each idea more closely.

Accept fears as normal. If you react strongly to your child's fears, they will tend to increase. Then your child may become even more fearful. Instead, be matter-of-fact: "I know the noisy vacuum is scary. But it won't hurt you, and it helps me get the rug clean."

Understand why your child is fearful. Fear may allow your child to control a situation, withdraw, or not take part. A preschooler can sometimes use fear to get attention or power. Sometimes, too, fear can be a sign that your child is going to be *aggressive*—that your child may push, hit, or hurt someone. Reassure your child that there are positive ways to be strong and have control. One way is by learning to use words to express feelings.

Mom and her son Paulo are riding the bus to his first day of pre-school. Paulo is frowning and kicking the seat ahead of him. Mom says, "I can tell you're nervous to be starting a new school. But kicking the seat won't help. Why don't you tell me what you're thinking about while you kick?"

Paulo says, "I'm thinking about my sandbox and trucks. I want to stay home and play with them." Mom says, "There's a nice sandbox at the school. And you can play in it with other kids. Won't that be fun?" "I don't wanna go," says Paulo. "It's strange to start somewhere new," Mom answers. "I wonder if some of the other kids feel funny about it too?"

Maintain limits. When your child is afraid, don't change your limits. By accepting these limits, your child will learn to develop courage. Courage is the positive alternative—the flip side—to fear. There are many ways to help a child overcome or lessen fear.

Nils is 4. He has grown scared of the dark. He refuses to go to bed. His parents are upset about this. So they have stretched their limits. They now allow Nils to sleep with them each night.

Nils's parents aren't helping their son cope with the fear. He may be sleeping soundly in his parents' bed. But he isn't building courage or confidence in himself. How can these parents help Nils overcome or lessen his fear?

- They could let him keep a light or night-light on in his room when he goes to sleep.

- They could explore the room before bed. Together, they could make sure there are no "monsters" in the closet or under the bed.

- They could suggest he sleep with a special toy animal to keep him company.

Over time, they can also talk with Nils. They can learn why he is afraid. They can help him decide if his fears make sense. It takes time to help children sort what *is* real from what *isn't.*

Help your child find outlets for strong feelings. Share how you, family members, and friends handle your feelings. Introduce your child to sports, games, music, drawing, and other activities that can help children express their feelings.

Some Common Fears

Two of young children's most common fears are of animals and nightmares.

Fears are normal. Teach ways to handle them.

Fear of animals. A child can get over some fear of animals by being around them. Let your child learn to play carefully with pets. Take the child to the zoo to see different animals. You might also help your child learn more about animals by reading books about them together. Go slowly. Forcing children to get too close if they aren't ready won't help them.

Nightmares. Frequent nightmares may be a sign that a child is upset about something. A night-light or listening to the child talk about the dream may be helpful.

Parent Fears

Watching their children grow, parents sometimes develop their own fears. They may feel anxious as their children explore the world. But a child can't remain a baby. Parents need to encourage growth, not stifle it.

For many years to come, you will encourage independence and set limits. Doing both is necessary. As you encourage your child to grow, you'll begin to see the child gain maturity and independence. This can help you grow more sure of yourself and your child.

Temper Tantrums

One of a child's most upsetting emotional behaviors is a temper tantrum. Temper tantrums can leave a parent feeling angry, out of control, and embarrassed.

There are two types of tantrums:

- frustration tantrums
- power tantrums

Parents can respond to each in a different way.

Frustration Tantrums

A young child may be unable to express feelings in words. Or a young child may find a task hard to do. The child's sense of failure and rage explodes into a tantrum.

Letting the child cry out this kind of tantrum is best. In fact, trying to stop it often makes things worse. When the tantrum is over, hold and comfort the child: "It's hard to want to do something so much and you can't. But someday you'll be able to do it."

Temper tantrums are hard on both parents and children.

Power Tantrums

A child may throw a tantrum to gain power. The child may be trying to force a parent to give in. Or revenge may be the point of the tantrum. If your child throws this type of tantrum, what can you do?

Ignore the tantrum. Ignoring this kind of tantrum is best. If possible, leave the room. Don't attempt to comfort or talk to the child. Doing so may reinforce the actions.

Use a time-out. Use time-out if ignoring the behavior isn't possible. Later, when the child has calmed down, talk about the feelings: "You were feeling very angry."

Give choices. Try offering alternatives.

Brenda is 2. She has started using tantrums to fight going to bed. If her parents leave the room and ignore the tantrums, Brenda will have what she wants––she won't go to bed.

So Brenda's parents offer her a choice: "Brenda, it's time for bed. You may choose to walk to your bed or be carried there." Then Brenda walks or is carried directly to bed. The tantrum may continue. But Brenda's parents haven't reinforced Brenda's goal of power.

Stopping Tantrums

Some temper tantrums can be ignored and they will stop. But other tantrums happen more and more. Don't allow these tantrums to continue. Often, the child is seeking a limit––asking to be stopped.

Pick up the child. Take the child to another room. Hold the child gently but firmly and say, "You can stay here until you stop _____." Be clear about what behavior you won't accept. Give the child five or ten minutes to calm down. Then bring the child back to the other room.

If the tantrum begins again, follow up promptly in the same way. Consistency and persistence are very important in stopping tantrums.

Preventing Tantrums

We can do many things to reduce tantrums. But we probably can't stop them completely.

Children often act aggressively when they are tired. If tantrums tend to happen when your child is tired, hungry, overexcited, or frustrated:

- Steer the child away from activities the child cannot do.

- Be aware of times when your child gets tired or hungry.

- Distract your child from a situation that might be tense.

- Help your child get rid of tension by running, jumping, or moving to music.

Stress

All young children have stress in their lives. Here are some ways you can help control stress at home:

- Listen to your child's feelings.

- Reduce competitiveness. Help your child learn to do well without comparing self to others.

- Encourage your child's efforts and notice any signs of progress.

- Create an atmosphere in which each child feels accepted.

- Help your child contribute to the family (for example, by doing chores).

- Help your child learn simple ways to relax (such as taking a deep breath).

Some children express tension physically: they might have headaches, or stomachaches that don't go away. Not all physical symptoms are caused by stress, though. Take your child to the doctor if:

- any of the symptoms persist

- pain is sharp, gets worse, or happens often

- the child vomits

- the child is dizzy or has vision problems

Understanding Social Development

As children grow, they become more independent. They begin to test their ideas in play and relationships. Maturing socially involves learning to deal with limits. When a parent uses consequences to set limits, the child learns the limits.

Tantrums usually happen when a child is tired, hungry, overexcited, or frustrated.

Along with parents' limits, children want independence.

Along with parents' limits, children want independence. Playing with other children lets them "test" themselves socially. As they get older, children become more interested in working and playing with others.

Preschoolers Are Learning to Be Social

Between the ages of 3 and 5, children work and play with others more than ever. They begin to learn social rules—what is acceptable and what is not.

Besides setting limits, parents need to encourage children's positive behavior. For example, instead of saying "Don't fight anymore!" a parent can say, "We need to be nice to people."

Age Differences

There are differences in preschoolers' social skills. Generally, the differences are due to age.

Three Year Olds

- Three year olds are learning to take turns. You may need to help measure their turns with a timer.

- They are also learning to share. When there is one toy, children need to share it. You can say, "Willis, when you're through playing with the truck, please give it to Lyn. She would like to play with it." Also let your 3 year old have a few special toys that don't need to be shared. These can be put away when other children come to play.

- At 3, children still enjoy playing alone. Don't force a child to play with other children. Let the child play *alongside* them.

Four Year Olds

- Four year olds have a great desire to play with other children. Your child may want to be at a friend's home or have the friend over all the time.

- They have active imaginations. They often create imaginary friends—human beings or animals. Play along with your child and these make-believe friends.

- They are determined. They can be bossy. They want to rely on themselves and may even appear able to do so.

- Five year olds are becoming more settled, more serious, more sure of themselves.

- They are developing positive feelings about their families.

- They are growing in their ability to cooperate.

Ways to Encourage Social Interest

One of the most important tasks of parents is teaching *social interest* to children. Social interest is caring about others and being willing to cooperate. It is based on respect. Here are some suggestions for teaching social interest.

Encourage helping at an early age. Offer chores that match your child's abilities. Comment aloud about the importance of helping:

- "It's nice when someone helps with the dishes."

- "It feels good to help Grandpa, doesn't it?"

Let children handle their own mistakes. As much as possible, let your children take care of their own mistakes. Children can pick up things they've dropped. They can clean up what they've spilled. In these ways, they learn the value of cooperation.

Don't expect perfection. Accept your child's efforts to do a task. This allows your child to feel free to take part, rather than hold back.

Recognize efforts and progress. Encouragement is a wonderful way to build your child's interest in the world! An encouraged child will continue to reach out for new experiences.

Don't change a child's first result. Don't remake the bed just because your child left some wrinkles and lumps. Criticism can take away a cooperative spirit.

Play, work, and learn together. Have your child take part in family, religious, and community activities. Include your child in family meetings, in helping others, and in projects like painting or cleaning.

Special Concerns About Social Development

Social development involves many things. Five concerns of special interest to most parents are honesty, aggression, toilet training, bedtime, and mealtime.

Honesty

We all want our children to be honest. With the preschool years, children often begin to say and do things that seem *dis*honest. But exaggerating and making up stories are typical behavior for preschoolers.

Often, children are telling us what they *wish* were true: "Look at me! I'm the strongest woman in the world!"

Children also lie for the same reasons adults do. They want to get a good result or avoid a bad one. But young children don't see anything wrong with telling a lie to get what they want.

If your child lies, don't overreact. Explain that it's important to tell the truth: "When I hear a story that isn't true, I feel worried. We need to talk about what really happened." Sometimes, too, you may simply choose to ignore lying.

Aggression

We've all heard of bullies. *Bully* is a name people commonly call children who use aggression to get what they want. As parents, we will probably have to deal with aggression at some time—from other children, or from our own.

When another child is aggressive. Children need to learn what choices they have when someone bullies them. For example:

- Your child may have to avoid playing with the aggressive child.

- You may have to send the aggressive child away.

- Your child may need to decide what he or she *will* and *will not* accept. You can help your child figure this out. Then your child will need to face the other child and refuse to be a victim.

- You can start by helping your child develop courage at home.

When your child is aggressive. If your child threatens other children, you need to understand the purpose of the behavior. It may be for power or control. Help your child reach the goals in a more

Exaggerating and making up stories are typical behavior for preschoolers.

acceptable way. What if the child continues to bully? Then the child is choosing not to play with other children. If your child continues bullying, you may need to talk to a counselor.

Toilet Training

Trying to toilet train a child too soon frustrates both the child and the parents. Most children aren't physically able to control their bowel or bladder until the age of 2 or later. Wait until your child is at least 2 before you start toilet training. If it doesn't work, wait a few weeks, then try again. Then there will be less stress for both you and your child. Be alert to your child's individual rhythms. It's important not to push a child through any of the stages of toilet training.

Here are some basic steps when toilet training your child:

Give your child words. Names for bowel movements and urination help the child understand what you are talking about. You might say: "Chandra is making a BM in her diaper."

Recognize success. Recognition can get the process started and keep it going. Equally important, don't scold your child for accidents or mistakes.

Make a potty seat available. Your child may want to copy other people's use of the toilet. When this happens, the child may be ready for a potty seat.

Make one available. Watch for a few days. See if your child shows an interest in using it. At first, encourage sitting on it in a once-a-day routine. Don't pressure the child by expecting results. Then have the child sit on the seat a few times a day. Try to do this at times during the day when your child usually wets or soils a diaper.

Offer training pants. Be sure your child uses the potty seat successfully for a few weeks. Training pants are the next step. If you rush this step, your child may feel afraid—even terrified.

Be cheerful about mistakes and setbacks. Accidents happen. You can put on clean pants and try again. Bladder control usually comes sooner then bowel control. Daytime control happens sooner than nighttime control.

Help your child avoid bed-wetting. You might say: "Let's not drink a glass of water just before bedtime." Don't wake your child for a trip to the bathroom. Doing so *pressures* the child and *takes away* the responsibility for getting up.

Don't push a child through any of the stages of toilet training.

Toddlers and preschoolers often dislike going to bed.

Be patient. Toilet training takes time. Most children will be toilet trained by their third birthday. It usually takes boys longer to achieve control than girls. Treat temporary setbacks as unfortunate, not as big mistakes. Help your child get clean and dry. Show sensitivity and interest: "You must really be uncomfortable."

Bedtime

Young children need plenty of sleep and regular rest periods. They need a set bedtime and a regular, pleasant ritual for going to sleep. These have a positive effect on behavior. They are needed for children's healthy development.

Many babies go to sleep willingly and regularly, as they feel the need. Often you can help even a fussy infant to sleep simply by stroking the baby's back for a while.

As they become toddlers and preschoolers, children often dislike going to bed. They may resist bedtime by demanding a drink, a hug, a trip to the bathroom, or one more story. They may want to discuss some imaginary problem or fear. They may have slept too long or too late during an afternoon nap.

Here are some ideas to help make bedtime simpler:

Talk about it earlier in the day. Say that you know your child is old enough to sleep alone. Explain that you won't be staying with your child at bedtime.

Start naps early in the afternoon. Don't let a nap last more than an hour and a half.

Plan ahead. Think about what your child's bedtime demands will be. Provide them before the child asks. Then tell the child kindly and firmly that this is the final good-night. Follow through.

Say, "This is the last story." Tell your child in advance that a story or a song is the last one and that you will be leaving the room.

Don't be available. Put your child to bed. Then don't respond to any additional calls for attention before the child goes to sleep.

What if a child wakes up crying and won't stay in bed?

- Make sure your child isn't seriously frightened or sick, doesn't need a diaper change, and isn't thirsty.

- Put your child back in bed and leave the room. Don't lie down with the child. Don't put the child in your bed.

- Repeat this process as many times as necessary. Do so firmly, kindly, and patiently. You'll need to do it fewer and fewer times each night.

Mealtime

Mealtime can set the stage for a young child to make a bid for power. Here are some ways to make mealtime less of a struggle.

Have regular mealtimes and snacktimes. Avoid giving snacks at unusual times. Rather than cookies or sugary drinks, provide healthy snacks. fruit, milk, or fruit juice.

Keep a reasonable time frame. Expect a young child to spend no more than fifteen or twenty minutes at the table. After that, the child may be excused and the food put away.

Provide small amounts of food. When the child has eaten the small amounts of food you provide, offer more. If the child begins to play with the food, the meal has come to an end. Say, "I see you've decided you're done eating."

Don't make food an issue. Avoid emphasizing food in your relationship with your child. Don't offer food as a reward or insist on a clean plate. These can set the stage for food to become a power struggle.

Fix a variety of foods for different meals. Consider what each person in your family likes. But don't get in the habit of fixing only certain foods. Don't start a pattern of making special meals for one family member or another. Doing these things gives children attention and power—not good nutrition.

Limit sweets. Have rules about when and in what amount sweets can be eaten. Avoid sweets yourself, and don't keep them in the cupboard. By doing so, you'll probably have fewer problems with this issue.

The Courage to Meet Challenges

Much of *Parenting Young Children* is really about courage. We want our children to develop courage—to be willing to meet challenges and solve them.

Courage isn't just for our children. Raising children is a challenge, and parents need courage to face that challenge successfully.

Encouragement
STEP

Encouraging yourself is just as important as encouraging your child. When you feel encouraged, you lose your fear or failure. You see your abilities more clearly. One way to encourage yourself is to think, write, and believe ideas such as:

- **I am a positive person.**
- **I am a capable person.**
- **I am capable of change.**
- **I love myself.**

Think about these encouraging ideas. What do they mean to you? What else can you say to yourself? Think of other encouraging ideas that apply to you.

Remind yourself of these beliefs. Write them down and post them on a mirror. Or keep them in your wallet or purse.

You have learned many ways to help your child grow. You help by:

- showing love and respect for your child and yourself
- understanding your child's development
- having realistic expectations
- encouraging your child
- listening and talking about feelings
- setting limits and giving choices

All of these skills and approaches take time and practice. Stick with it. Be patient with yourself and your child. When you have trouble, think about your parenting goals:

- to raise a child who is happy, healthy, self-reliant, respectful, confident, cooperative, and responsible
- to build a strong, lifelong relationship with your child
- to help your child grow to be a responsible adult
- to raise a child who is loved and able to give love

With all these actions, you are building children's courage. Together, these are the most loving gifts you can give your child.

POINTS TO REMEMBER

1. Be aware of and sensitive to your child's feelings. Set appropriate limits. Recognize that older toddlers and preschoolers may use feelings to get attention, power, or revenge or to display inadequacy.

2. Young children use crying to express their feelings and needs. They may also use crying to control parents.

3. Sadness may be a response to a loss. It can also be a way to cope with other feelings. Listen and show you understand. Help the child be aware of the feelings.

4. Jealousy can be especially strong in toddlers and young preschoolers. It most often occurs when a new baby arrives in the family.

5. To help your child handle fears and anxieties:
   - Accept fears as normal.
   - Understand why your child is fearful.
   - Maintain limits.
   - Use your reflective listening skills.

6. Some temper tantrums come from frustration. Let the child cry out this kind of tantrum. Then comfort the child. Other temper tantrums are for power. Ignore these tantrums or use a time-out.

7. All young children have stress in their lives. They may express tension through physical symptoms. But not all physical symptoms are due to stress.

8. Preschoolers are learning to be sociable. Set limits, but also focus on children's positive behavior. Teach your child to care about, help, and cooperate with others.

9. Lying and exaggerating are normal for preschoolers. Don't overreact to lying.

10. If your child is bullied, he or she needs to learn what choices there are in dealing with the aggressive child. If your child is aggressive, understand the purpose of the behavior. Help your child reach goals in a more acceptable way.

11. Don't try to toilet train a child before the age of 2. Be patient—toilet training takes time.

12. A set bedtime and a regular, pleasant bedtime ritual have a positive effect on children's behavior.

13. Don't let mealtime become a power struggle between you and your child.

JUST FOR YOU

Fighting Negative Beliefs

Beliefs cause feelings. If you choose to think of unpleasant things, you will have unpleasant feelings. How you feel results from what you think. Negative beliefs cause problems. They get in the way of your happiness.

Your discouraging words and self-talk show your beliefs. They sound like demanding, blaming, and complaining:

- "I *should* be perfect."
- "I *should* be the best."
- "I *must* win."
- "I *must* succeed."
- "I *need* to be in control."
- "I *need* to please everyone."
- "I *should* be right."
- "I *should* make a good impression."
- "People *should* give me my own way."
- "People *should* recognize my contribution."
- "Life *should* be fair."
- "Life *should* be easy."

Learn to think positive, more effective thoughts:

- Choose new thoughts.
- Look at negative situations in a logical way.
- Look at "wants" and "wishes," not "shoulds" and "musts."
- See "catastrophes" as the simple disappointments that they are.

To fight negative beliefs, ask yourself:

1. What am I thinking? Am I demanding or blaming?
2. Does my belief make sense? How do I know this?
3. What will happen if I hang on to these beliefs?
4. What will happen if I change my beliefs?

Chart 7

MY PLAN FOR MEETING MY PARENTING CHALLENGES

Child's name: _____

Challenge 1: _____

What I've been doing about it: _____

_____

My beliefs that interfere with progress: _____

_____

My plan for meeting the challenge: _____

_____

_____

My progress: _____

_____

_____

Challenge 2: _____

What I've been doing about it: _____

_____

My beliefs that interfere with progress: _____

_____

My plan for meeting the challenge: _____

_____

_____

My progress: _____

_____

_____

INDEX